BECOMING VEGETARIAN
by Mary Donovan

BECOMING VEGETARIAN

For information contact IronRingPublishing.com

ISBN-13: 978-1523885336

ISBN-10: 1523885335

First Edition: February 2016

10 9 8 7 6 5 4 3 2 1

Table of Contents

Introduction

Depending on where you live, you no doubt have come across someone who doesn't eat meat. In some places it is commonplace, but in others it can raise some eyebrows. Meat has always played a big part in American culture and economy, but in 2015, 5% of the population was reported to be either vegetarian or vegan. This means that about 16 million people in the US do not eat meat! Why this incredible leap? What has transformed the steak-eating cowboy into a kale-munching cosmopolite?

Plenty of actors, athletes, TV hosts, and other high-profile individuals confess their aversion for meat. There are certainly many reasons why people turn away from meat or animal by-products. One of the biggest reasons has to do with the ethical treatment of animals. Some people are vegetarian because of the health benefits; others have given up meat because of concern for the environment. Some choose not to eat meat simply because they do not like the taste, and others refuse animal products because of spiritual or religious reasons.

Vegetarian or Vegan?

It is said that vegetarianism is a diet while veganism is a lifestyle. The vegetarian does not eat meat but eats animal products like eggs and dairy. They may also use animal-based products like fur, wool, silk and leather. The vegan, on the other hand, shuns not only meat but animal products as well, such as milk and honey. This is because veganism is more of a philosophy that espouses compassion for living things. Vegans are against the use of animals and animal-products for food, clothing, cosmetics or pharmaceutics. Vegans have strong political advocacies for the protection and humane treatment of animals. It may be said that vegans have evolved from following a simple vegetarian diet to embracing a more committed and intense philosophy of veganism.

The Academy of Nutrition and Dietetics (AND) gives this classification:

Vegans exclude ALL animal products, both in diet and in other products.

Lacto vegetarians exclude meat, poultry, fish, and eggs but still consume dairy products.

Lacto-ovo vegetarians exclude meat, poultry and fish but include dairy products and eggs. There are also **pescetarians** who avoid meat and poultry, but consume fish and dairy products.

Both vegans and vegetarians make fruits, vegetables, legumes, grains and nuts their staples. They avoid "hidden" animal products like lard, gelatin (including gel capsules used for medicine), and beef or chicken stocks. Tofu and other soybean products are used as a source of protein.

Is it healthier?

There are health rewards to be reaped from following a vegetarian diet. The low fat, high fiber vegetarian or vegan diet results in less chances of developing heart disease, obesity, hypertension, diabetes or cancer (specifically ovarian, colorectal and breast cancers). Eating less meat also means less exposure to possible sources of food poisoning and residual antibiotics, chemicals, or hormones that were given to farm animals. Veganism helps eliminate food allergens such as dairy and shellfish. And, by substituting meat with high-fiber, nutrient-rich fruits, vegetables, beans, and whole grains, the body acquires more nutrients. Thus, you get a healthier, slimmer and more energetic body. Some athletes credit a no-meat diet to their enhanced performance and easy recovery from workouts. In general, vegetarians live longer and they will less likely succumb to heart disease.

Some argue that one can become just as healthy by simply making the right food choices, without giving up meat. But a number of people who have turned to vegetarianism say that their food choices have made it easy for them to resist eating refined and highly-processed food. If becoming a vegetarian makes it so easy to give up fast food and junk, then it's definitely the best choice for better health.

Some important nutrition concerns

As much as a vegetarian diet can be healthful and full of benefits, there is still the possibility of suffering from lack of nutrients. Most vegetarians are health-conscious and careful with the food they eat. But even a vegetarian diet can be unhealthy if it includes too much fat- and sugar-rich foods. A good vegetarian diet should be well-planned and well-balanced to ensure that all nutritional needs are met. Vegetarians have to be especially careful to meet their protein, vitamin B12, iron, zinc, calcium, and vitamin D requirements.

Protein

There are many plant foods that contain protein. The average adult needs 0.4-0.5 grams of protein per pound for the body to perform healthily. This requirement can obtained through the proper balance of plant-based proteins. Lentils, beans, tofu, soybeans, nuts, seeds, tempeh and eggs are good sources of protein. The key is variety. Particular emphasis is placed on tofu because it is a soybean product. Soybean is known as a complete protein, meaning it contains all essential amino acids. Toby McGuire, the actor who played Spiderman, is a vegetarian who credits his bulk to eating tofu.

Vitamin B12

Vegans are especially at risk of being deficient in vitamin B12 (also called cobalamin). This vitamin is important in the synthesis of DNA and red blood cells. Animals and bacteria produce this vitamin. It is present in dairy products and eggs. For vegans, including foods such as tempeh and seaweed, along with vitamin B12 supplements, can help prevent deficiency.

Iron, calcium, and zinc
Low-fat or fat-free dairy products are rich sources of calcium. Vegans can avail of calcium from dark leafy greens such as spinach and kale. Calcium may also be availed of from calcium-fortified juices or cereals. Iron is also abundant in dark greens as well as dried fruits, molasses, seeds, and fortified cereals. Using iron pots in cooking can also fortify your food. Legumes, nuts, seeds and oatmeal are good sources of zinc. Zinc is better absorbed in tandem with protein. So consuming plant protein will help ensure the sufficiency of zinc in the body. Leavened bread and supplementation is also recommended.

Vitamin D
Vitamin D is present in sunlight and helps the body absorb calcium. US dairy products and many soy products are fortified with this vitamin. To absorb vitamin D from sunlight, one needs at least 10 minutes of exposure. For people who do not receive direct sun exposure or who don't consume dairy products, supplements should be considered.

The First Steps To Becoming A Vegetarian

The information given has most probably convinced you to try vegetarianism. You may want to because you love animals, or you care for the environment. Maybe you want to have a healthier, stronger and slimmer body. Whatever your reasons, here are some tips to help you become a vegetarian:

1. **Find your motivation**. A famous singer and actress became a vegetarian the moment she visited a slaughterhouse. She didn't need to have religious or deep ideological reasons; she just didn't want to participate in any form of cruelty to animals. You'll need to have your own motivation. Is it for good health and long life? To help save the planet? For religious reasons? You may have a petty or even silly reason, but it's is still YOUR motivation and it will keep you going.

2. **Don't go cold turkey.** This may have worked for some, but you have a greater chance of success if you do things gradually. Suddenly depriving yourself of what your body is used to will set you up for cravings and sure failure. If you drop things a step at a time, you'll eventually find that you no longer have any desire for any kind of meat. Most people start by dropping red meat. You can drop it one meal at a time, or drop red meat this month and then pork the next month. It's

all up to you. Doing it gradually will train your body to lose its interest meat. Soon, you'll find it easy to give up poultry and fish. It will come naturally.

3. **Make it an adventure.** Try new recipes, new ingredients, learn new cultures. Visit health food stores and see what products they have. Try out some vegetarian restaurants. Look for recipes on the internet. Find interesting substitutes for the ingredients you're familiar with. Have you tried a banana-blossom burger? How about a tofu tiramisu for dessert? There are many Chinese, Ethiopian, Indian and Greek vegetarian dishes. It can be an adventure that will introduce you to many worlds.

4. **Tell your loved ones**. It will help you especially because they'll be inviting you to parties, dinners and social gatherings. Don't make it like an aggressive stand that you have to defend. It will just help so you don't find yourself at a gathering with nothing suitable to eat. They'll understand if you have to bring your own food, or they might even prepare something for you. You will need their loving support to achieve success.

5. **Do some planning**. Without planning, you might find yourself in a situation where you realize you have nothing to eat and you'll be forced to eat something

you're not supposed to. You can cook ahead to make sure you have meals for a few days or a week. Pack your own lunch, or have some healthy snacks ready. Have cereals, grains, beans (canned or dry), tofu, whole wheat crackers, bread, rice, pasta, tortillas, nuts, fruit (canned or frozen), yogurt and soy products stocked up in your pantry.

6. **Don't be too hard on yourself**. Don't make this change in your diet too traumatic. Go easy on yourself and allow yourself a little more carbs, cheese of processed vegetarian food. Once in a while is okay. Knowing that you've "cheated" a little could motivate you to try even harder the next time.

7. **Learn more.** While you're taking your steps to changing your food choices, don't stop at getting more information. Read books on vegetarianism. Watch movies. Many say they became vegetarians after watching a movie about it. Read testimonials about people who became vegetarians and how they benefitted from it. This way, you will not feel alone in your journey.

Going Vegan

Most vegans started out as vegetarians. Vegetarians are more after a healthy diet, but veganism is more of a lifestyle and philosophy. There are countless reasons to go vegan, and the moral and environmental arguments for veganism are solid.

Whether you are interested in veganism because of the health benefits, environmental concerns, compassion for animals, ethics, or you simply want to try new and tasty dishes, this cookbook could be your invaluable guide. With this cookbook, you'll find it easy to prepare delicious, nutritionally-balanced, and exciting dishes. The recipes range from easy to intricate, but you're sure to find something that suits you.

One of the myths about vegan food is that it's expensive. If you check out the recipes here, you'll discover many simple, money-saving but equally tasty dishes. Some recipes may seem extravagant but, in the long term, the health benefits will outweigh the cost. Many vegans have done away with a big chunk of their expenses on medical bills because they have become so fit and healthy, they rarely ever get sick.

The recipes here are easy to follow, with step-by-step instructions and cooking tips. You'll find all kinds to choose from for breakfast, lunch, dinner and snacks. Another advantage to being vegan is doing away with a messy, drawn-out and complicated processes associated with cooking meat and meat products. Cooking vegan recipes can sometimes be done in just 15 minutes! Nutrition information is also given so you can carefully watch you calorie, fat, sodium or sugar intake.

This cookbook is for newcomers and old-timers alike. One of the great things about vegan cooking is the myriad of modification that can be done on a single recipe. You can substitute soymilk with coconut, almond or rice milk, for example. Instead of rice, you can use quinoa or cauliflower. You can come up with your own unique combinations and personalized creations – and all of them with wonderful health benefits. Of course, the results will have various interesting textures and flavor profiles.

A vegan dish is an expression of love – for one's own well-being, for other living creatures and for the planet we live in. It is a cleansing, detoxifying experience. As you consume nutrient-dense, fiber-rich food, you rid your body of toxins, build up immunity and rev up your system. The result is a healthier, stronger and happier you!

Vegan cooking is meant to be shared with family and friends. It's time to feast on what will not only satisfy the taste buds but the body's needs as well. The body needs food that is whole, natural, cleansing, nourishing and satisfying. Instead of taxing the body's system, vegan food conditions and heals.
You are invited to embark on a journey to health and well-being with never a dull moment! The

dishes you will make will inundate your senses with new flavors, exotic ingredients and unusual textures. You will feel that supercharge of energy that the body craves. It's time to give your body what it deserves – good food that satisfies its nutritional and energy requirements. Vegan cuisine is holistic – it feeds, not only the body, but the soul as well.

BREAKFAST RECIPES

Vegan Cheese and Spinach Scramble

Yield: 1 serving

Ingredients

3 egg whites

2 cups spinach, chopped

1 medium tomato, chopped

1/4 cup onion, chopped

1/4 cup feta cheese, crumbled, divided

salt & pepper to taste

Directions

1. Coat a skillet with cooking spray and sauté onion over medium heat.
2. When onions are translucent, add egg whites, tomato, and spinach. Stir over heat until cooked through.
3. Put in half of the feta cheese and cook until just melted.
4. Season with salt and pepper.
5. Serve topped with the remaining feta cheese.

Nutrition Information

Serving size: 1
Calories: 200
Total Fat: 8.7 g
Total Carbohydrate: 13 g
Sugars: 0.7 g
Protein: 18.4 g
Sodium: 615 mg

Indian Chickpea"Omelet" (Besan Cheela)

Yield: 2 omelets

Ingredients

3/4 cup besan or chickpea flour (also called gram flour)

1/2 teaspoon cumin seeds

Salt and pepper to taste

1/2 cup water

1/2 small onion, chopped

1 small tomato, seeded and chopped

1 large mushroom, sliced finely

1 cup spinach, chopped

1/4 cup coriander leaves, chopped

2 Tablespoons coconut oil

Directions

1. Mix all dry ingredients (the first 3) in a bowl.

2. Add water and stir until smooth. It should look like pancake batter.
3. Add the onion, tomato, mushroom, spinach and coriander. Stir.
4. Heat a non-stick pan and pour in about 1/2 cup batter.
5. Starting from the center outwards in a circular motion, use the back of a ladle to spread the batter into a circle of about 7-inch diameter.
6. When the edges begin to separate from the pan and the batter starts to dry, spread 2 teaspoon of oil over it. Cook half a minute longer.
7. Flip the 'omelet' over and press down to cook evenly. Flip over 1 or 2 times more. The omelet is done when golden brown.
8. Cook the rest of the batter the same way.

Nutrition Information

Serving size: 1 omelet
Calories: 292
Total Fat: 16.5 g
Total Carbohydrate: 28.4 g
Sugars: 4.3 g
Protein: 10.5 g
Sodium:404 mg

Vegan Waffles

Yield: 5

Ingredients

2 cups all-purpose flour

1 cup whole wheat flour

2 Tablespoons baking soda

1/8 teaspoon salt

1/2 cup applesauce

2 1/2 cups soymilk

2 Tablespoons canola oil

Directions

1. Preheat waffle iron.
2. Combine dry ingredients in a large bowl.
3. In another bowl, whisk,wet ingredients together.
4. Make a "well" in the dry ingredients. Pour in about half of the wet ingredients and mix.
5. Add the rest of the liquid and whisk batter until free from lumps.

6. Coat the waffle iron with non-stick cooking spray or brush with oil. Pour in some of the batter.
7. Cook until waffles are golden brown.
8. Serve hot.

Nutrition Information

Serving size: 2 waffles
Calories: 200
Total Fat: 4.3 g
Total Carbohydrate: 33.9 g
Sugars: 3.8 g
Protein: 5.9 g
Sodium: 294 mg

Kale and Strawberry Smoothie

Yield: 1-2 servings

Ingredients

3/4 cup frozen strawberries.

1/2 cup cucumber, peeled and sliced

1 large frozen banana, cut into about 4 pieces

1 1/2 cup vanilla almond milk

1 1/2 cups kale, loosely packed, stems removed

1/2 cup spinach

Ice, if desired

Directions

1. Blend almond milk, banana and kale on high.
2. Add strawberries and cucumber. Blend well.
3. Consistency may be adjusted with more almond milk and ice.
4. Serve.

Nutrition Information

Serving size: 1 serving
Calories: 295
Total Fat: 5.1 g
Total Carbohydrate: 62.5 g
Sugars: 37.9 g
Protein: 7.4 g
Sodium: 286 mg

Spicy Oat Pancakes (Dosa)

Yield: 2 pancakes

Ingredients

1/2 cup quick-cooking oats

1/4 cup whole wheat flour

1/8 teaspoon baking soda

1/8 teaspoon cumin powder

1/4 teaspoon salt

2 Tablespoons low-fat yogurt, plain

1/2 cup water

1/4 cup onions,minced

1 small carrot, grated

1/2 cup tomato,seeded, very finelychopped

1 tablespoon cilantro, finely chopped

1 teaspoon green chili, chopped (optional)

Non-stick cooking spray, if needed

Directions

1. Combine first five ingredients in a bowl.
2. Whisk in yogurt and water until smooth.
3. Add the rest of the ingredients and mix well.
4. Into preheated non-stick pan (or a greased skillet), pour some of the batter. Spread out the batter in circular motion to make a thin pancake or crepe.
5. When edges begin to dry, flip over. Press down to cook evenly.
6. Flip over and press down a few times until golden brown.
7. Traditionally served with chutney or vegetable curry.

Nutrition Information

Serving size: 1-2 pancakes
Calories: 198
Total Fat:2.8 g
Total Carbohydrate: 335.9 g
Sugars:5 g
Protein: 8.3 g
Sodium:435 mg

Radish Flatbread (Mooli Paratha)

Yield: 4 pieces

Ingredients

For Filling

2 cups white radish, shredded

1/2 Tablespoon salt

1/2 teaspoon carom (also called ajwain) seeds

1 teaspoon green chili,minced

2 tablespoons cilantro, finely chopped

For Dough

1 cup whole wheat flour + 1/4 cup for rolling the dough

1/2 teaspoon salt

6 tablespoonsvegetable oil, divided

1/2 cup water

Directions

For Filling

(This should be done just before making the flatbread.)

1. Mix shredded radish with salt. Mash or mix thoroughly for about 3 minutes.
2. Squeeze the radish to remove its 'juice' or liquid.
3. Add the other ingredients for the filling. Mix well.

For Dough

1. Combine flour,saltand 1 tablespoon oil (the rest of the oil will be used while cooking the paratha) in a bowl. Add water gradually, while mixing, until a soft dough is achieved.
2. Knead on an oiled surface for a minute or until pliable.
3. Let sit for 10 minutes.
4. Divide the dough equally into 4 pieces.
5. Shape one piece into a rough ball and press the edges to form a small circle of about 3 inches in diameter. Edges should be thinner than the center.
6. Place a little of the filling in the center and fold the edges over to cover it. Pinch gently to seal.

7. Place flour for rolling in a plate or tray. Press both sidesof the filled dough into the flour.
8. Sealed side up, use a rolling pin to flatten the dough further to about 6 inches diameter.Dust with flour to prevent sticking.
9. Cook in a pre-heated skillet over medium heat (non-stick is advisable especially for beginners). Flip the paratha over when it begins to brown slightly.
10. Spread about a teaspoon of oil over the paratha and flip over again. Press down to cook evenly. Keep flipping and pressing until both sides are golden brown.
11. Cook the remaining parathas.
12. Best served hot.

Nutrition Information

Serving size: 1 flatbread or paratha
Calories: 140
Total Fat: 5 g
Total Carbohydrate: 7 g
Sugars: 1g
Protein: 10 g
Sodium: 100 mg

Oatmeal and Blueberry Waffles

Yield: 6

Ingredients

1 cup white whole wheat flour, sifted

1 tablespoon baking powder

1/2 teaspoon salt

1/4 teaspoon ground allspice

1 cup quick cooking oats

1/3 cup applesauce, unsweetened

1 1/2 cups dairy milk substitute (like almond milk or rice milk)

3 tablespoons maple syrup

2 tablespoons canola oil

1 teaspoon vanilla

1 1/2 cups frozen blueberries

Directions

1. Combine all dry (first 4) ingredients in a bowl. Stir in oats.
2. Make a well in the center and pour in applesauce, maple syrup, oil and vanilla.

3. Mix until free of lumps. Rest the batter for at least 5 minutes.
4. Add blueberries and mix to distribute. Don't overmix.
5. Cook waffles (about 1/2 cup batter at a time) in a pre-heated, greased waffle iron until golden brown.

Nutrition Information

Serving size: 6
Calories: 203.5
Total Fat: 3.7 g
Total Carbohydrate: 39.1g
Sugars: 10.8 g
Protein: 4.8 g
Sodium: 487 mg

Quinoa Breakfast Bowl

Yield: 4 bowls

Ingredients

1 cup organic quinoa, rinsed

1 cup low fat soy milk

1 cup water

2 cups fresh blackberries

1/2 teaspoon ground cinnamon

1/3 cup chopped pecans, toasted

4 teaspoons choice of sweetener(like agave nectar, maple syrup, or honey)

Directions

1. Combine quinoa, soy milk and water in a saucepan. Cook over high heat to bring to a boil.
2. Reduce heat and simmer until most of the moisture is absorbs (about 15 minutes).
3. Turn off heat. Allow to cook in residual heat 5-10 minutes longer.
4. Portion into 4 bowls.
5. Serve topped with pecans and syrup.

Nutrition Information

Serving size: 1 bowl
Calories: 235
Total Fat: 0.6 g
Total Carbohydrate: 34.8 g
Sugars: 11.9 g
Protein: 5.9 g
Sodium: 23.5 g

Breakfast Rice Flakes (Poha)

Yield: 4 servings

Ingredients

3 cups rice flakes (or Indian "poha"), soaked

1 Tablespoons coconut oil

1 teaspoon mustard seeds

1 teaspoon cumin seeds

3/4 cup onions, chopped

3/4 cup carrots, grated

3/4 cup tomatoes, seeded and chopped

1/2 cup peas

2 Thai peppers (also called Bird's Eye Chili)

1 teaspoon turmeric powder

1 teaspoon chili powder

1 Tablespoon salt

1 Tablespoon lemon juice

Directions

1. First, prepare the poha by rinsing 3-4 times and then soaking until soft (3-4 minutes). Drain and set aside.
2. In a frying pan, heat oil until almost at smoking point. Add the cumin and mustard seeds and cook until they start to

crackle (after about 25 seconds). Reduce heat. Sauté onion until translucent.
3. Add carrots, peas and tomatoes and sauté a few minutes longer until vegetables are tender.
4. Season with all the spices, chilies, and salt.
5. Add the pre-soaked and drained rice flakes and cook, with mixing, until heated through.
6. Serve squeezed with lemon juice.

Nutrition Information

Serving size: 1 serving
Calories: 270
Total Fat: 4.6 g
Total Carbohydrate: 51.3 g
Sugars: 5 g
Protein: 5.9 g
Sodium: 1765 mg

Japanese Breakfast Lentils

Yield: 8 servings

Ingredients

2 Tablespoons olive oil

1 medium leek, finely chopped

1 clove garlic, thinly sliced

1 tablespoon tomato paste

1 cup green canal house or French lentils

2 1/2 cups water

2 tablespoons soy sauce, reduced-sodium

Salt and pepper

Directions

1. In a saucepan, heat oil and sauté garlic and leek.
2. Add tomato paste and continue cooking until paste darkens.
3. Add water and lentils. Bring to a boil.
4. Simmer, covered, for 45 minutes or until lentils are tender.
5. Turn off heat. Leave covered and let stand for 10 mintues.

Season with soy sauce, salt and pepper.

Nutrition Information

Serving size: 1 serving
Calories: 110
Total Fat: 4 g
Total Carbohydrate: 16 g
Sugars: 4 g
Protein: 1 g
Sodium: 80 g

Hearty Breakfast Bars

Yield: 12 bars

Ingredients

1 cup dates, pitted and halved

1 1/2 cups apple juice

3 cups rolled oats, divided

1 large banana

1 teaspoon vanilla extract

3/4 teaspoon ground cinnamon

1/4 teaspoon ground nutmeg

1 1/2 tablespoons baking powder

1 cup blueberries (freshorfrozen)

1/2 cup walnuts, chopped

Directions

1. Soak the dates in apple juice for 15 minutes. Drain (do not throw away juice).
2. Preheat the oven to 375 degrees and prepare a 9×9-inch baking pan, lined with parchment paper.

3. In a blender, combine 1 cup oats, banana and vanilla extract. Pour in the apple juice (from soaked dates). Blend until creamy.
4. In a large bowl,mix together the remaining 2 cups oats, cinnamon, nutmeg and baking powder.
5. Make a well in the center and pour in the blended banana mixture. Mix until batter is lump-free.
6. Add blueberries and walnuts. Mix batter to evenly distribute berries and nuts.
7. Pour the batter into baking pan and bake for 30 to 35 minutes. A toothpick inserted into the center should come out clean.
8. Allow to cool for at least 10 minutes before cutting and serving.

Nutrition Information

Serving size: 1 bar
Calories: 216
Total Fat: 8.3 g
Total Carbohydrate: 34.3 g
Sugars: 12.8 g
Protein: 4.6 g
Sodium:63 mg

French Toast

Yield: 3 servings

Ingredients

1 cup almond milk

1 Tablespoon maple syrup

2 Tablespoons millet or whole wheat flour

1 Tablespoon nutritional yeast

1 teaspoon ground cinnamon

1/4 teaspoon ground nutmeg

A pinch of salt

6 slices ciabatta, day-old, sliced about 3/4-inch thick

1-2 Tablespoons coconut oil

Directions

1. Whisk the first 6 ingredients together.
2. Dip the bread slices into the almond milk mixture, making sure to coat them evenly.
3. Heat a skillet over medium heat and coat lightly with coconut oil.
4. Toast the bread slices, making sure to brown on both sides.
5. Serve sprinkled with powdered sugar, stevia or with your choice of syrup (maple, honey, agave, etc.) and fresh fruit.

Nutrition Information

Serving size: 1 piece
Calories: 176
Total Fat: 6.3 g
Total Carbohydrate: 27 g
Sugars: 4 g
Protein: 4.3 g
Sodium: 341 mg

Spiced Cream of Wheat

Yield: 2 servings

Ingredients

2 cups coconut milk

1/3 cup cream of wheat, whole grain

1 Tablespoon rose water (alternatives: 1 1/2 teaspoons vanilla or 1/2 teaspoon almond extract)

1/2 cup pistachios, finely chopped

1/2 teaspoon cardamom powder

3 Tablespoons Maple syrup or brown sugar (or stevia also may be substituted according to taste)

1 teaspoon coconut oil

Pistachio nuts for garnish

Directions

1. In a bowl, mix together cream of wheat, cardamom, pistachios and sugar. Set aside.
2. In a saucepan, bring coconut milk to a boil. Keep uncovered and stir constantly to prevent spilling.
3. Add rosewater to boiling coconut milk.

4. Add mixture of dry ingredients gradually, whisking continuously.
5. Adjust heat to low. Add coconut oil and simmer. Continue stirring while cooking for a few more minutes or until thickened.
6. Serve garnished with more pistachio nuts.

Nutrition Information

Serving size: 1 serving
Calories: 346
Total Fat: 17.5 g
Total Carbohydrate: 41.1 g
Sugars: 10 g
Protein: 9.4 g
Sodium: 190 mg

Polenta

Yield: 2 servings

Ingredients

2/3 cup fine grain polenta

1 clove garlic, minced

1 teaspoon extra virgin olive oil

2 cups vegetable broth

2 Tablespoons sun-dried tomatoes, chopped small

1/4 cup non-dairy milk (like rice, soy or almond)

1 Tablespoon nutritional yeast flakes

Salt and pepper

Directions

1. Heat olive oil in a small pot and sauté the garlic over medium heat until fragrant.
2. Add broth and bring to a boil.
3. Bring down to a simmer. While stirring constantly, gradually add polenta.
4. When polenta has thickened and pulls from the sides, add the rest of the

ingredients and mix thoroughly. Season with salt and pepper.

5. Serve. May be topped with roasted or sautéed vegetables, basil, beans or bell pepper.

Nutrition Information

Serving size: 1 serving
Calories: 269
Total Fat: 3.5 g
Total Carbohydrate: 51.4 g
Sugars: 3.3 g
Protein: 6.7 g
Sodium: 1170 mg

Breakfast Oat Morsels

Yield: 12 pieces

Ingredients

1 cup rolled oats

1 cup oat flour

1/3 cup raisins

1/4 cup finely shredded coconut, unsweetened

1 teaspoon baking powder

1 teaspoon cinnamon

1 tsp lemon or orange zest

1/4 teaspoon salt

A dash nutmeg

1/2 cup applesauce, unsweetened

1/4 cup maple syrup

3 tablespoons vegan chocolate chips (optional)

Directions

1. Preheat oven to 350 degrees.
2. Prepare a baking sheet lined with parchment paper.
3. In a bowl, combine oats, flour, raisins coconut, baking powder, cinnamon, zest, salt and nutmeg.
4. Add applesauce, maple syrup, and chocolate chips (optional).
5. Mix well and scoop by heaping tablespoon onto cookie sheet.
6. Bake for 15 minutes. Remove from oven and let cool for about a minute.
7. Transfer morsels to cooling rack.

Nutrition Information

Serving size: 1 morsel
Calories: 117
Total Fat: 2.5 g
Total Carbohydrate: 22.9 g
Sugars: 7.5 g
Protein: 3.1 g
Sodium: 91 mg

WRAPS, SANDWICHES, AND SPREADS

Pizza Sandwich

Yield: 1 sandwich

Ingredients

2 slices mixed grain bread

2 Tablespoons marinara sauce

1/4 mozarella cheese, low moisture, part-skim

1 teaspoon parmesan cheese, shredded

Salt and pepper

Directions

1. Spread marinara sauce on both slices of bread. Over one slice of bread, spread mozzarella and sprinkle with parmesan.
2. Close sandwich with other bread slice, sauce side down. Grill in a pan or oven until cheese has melted and bread is golden brown.

Nutrition Information

Serving size: 1 sandwich
Calories: 242
Total Fat: 8.3 g
Total Carbohydrate: 26.3 g
Sugars: 3.3 g
Protein: 15 g
Sodium: 557 mg

Veggie Burrito

Yield: 1 burrito

Ingredients

1 flour tortilla

1/2 cup black beans, precooked or canned

1 scrambled egg

1 Tablespoon light sour cream

2 Tablespoons salsa

2 Tablespoons cheddar cheese, shredded

Directions

1. Preheat oven to 350 degrees.
2. Cut out a sheet of aluminum foil a little larger in size than the tortilla.
3. Lay the tortilla on the sheet of foil.
4. Place beans and scrambled egg on the center of the tortilla.
5. Top with cheese and drizzle with sour cream and salsa.
6. Fold left and right sides toward, but not exactly at, the center.

7. Bring up the bottom flap of tortilla and roll upwards.
8. Moisten the top flap with a little water to help seal.
9. Wrap with foil the same way you wrapped the tortilla.
10. Heat in oven for 8-10 minutes.

Nutrition Information

Serving size: 1 burrito (about 235 g)
Calories: 563
Total Fat: 16.1 g
Total Carbohydrate: 74.7 g
Sugars: 3.6 g
Protein: 32.6 g
Sodium: 370 mg

Vegan Choco-Hazelnut Spread

Yield: 1 cup

Ingredients

1 1/2 cups hazelnuts, skinned

1-2 Tablespoons hazelnut oil (peanut or coconut oils will do, too)

3/4 cup powdered sugar

2 Tablespoons cocoa powder

2 Tablespoons soy powder

1/4 teaspoon vanilla

Directions

1. Toast the hazelnuts in oven for about 20 minutes at 350 degrees. Turn over frequently to avoid burning the nuts.
2. As soon as toasting is done, and while still hot, grind the hazelnuts in a blender. Add oil and vanilla and blend until a coarse butter.
3. Add the rest of the ingredients and continue blending. If needed, add more oil gradually.

4. Continue blending until desired consistency is reached.

Nutrition Information

Serving size: 1 Tablespoon
Calories: 115
Total Fat: 8.1 g
Total Carbohydrate: 10 g
Sugars: 8.3 g
Protein: 2.4 g
Sodium: 78 mg

Quick Vegan Meal-in-a-Sandwich

Yield: 1 sandwich

Ingredients

1 piece English muffin

1/2 teaspoon extra virgin olive oil

2 Tablespoons vegan sausage, formed into a patty

3 thin slices bell pepper

1 Tablespoon vegan cheese, shredded

1 teaspoon hot sauce (optional)

1/2 teaspoon vegan butter

1 teaspoon maple syrup of berry jam

pepper

Directions

1. Grill muffin, unsliced, on both sides.
2. Cut off around 2 tablespoons from a tube of vegan sausage. Using your hands, shape into a patty.
3. Rub the olive oil on the patty and grill. If using a skillet, press down with a spatula to cook through.
4. Slice the muffin and grill the inside parts. Grill the bell peppers as well.
5. Turn patty over and sprinkle cheese on it while still on the grill. Spread hot sauce on the cheese.
6. Spread vegan butter on inner side on one muffin and jam on the other.
7. Place patty with cheese between muffin slices, top with peppers and serve.
8. Other vegetables (such as spinach, tomato, cucumber, etc.) may also be used as topping for the patty, if desired.

Nutrition Information

Serving size: 1
Calories: 399
Total Fat: 21.5 g
Total Carbohydrate: 45.4 g
Sugars: 1.4 g
Protein: 9.6 g
Sodium: 978 mg

Mexican-inspired Vegan Toast

Yield: 2 pieces

Ingredients

2 slices of vegan sandwich bread (such as baguettes, pane francese and ciabatta)

1 cup refried beans

1 avocado, thinly sliced

White onion slivers for topping

Sea salt

Directions

1. Toast the bread.
2. Spread refried beans on toast.
3. Top with avocado and then onion slivers.
4. Sprinkle with sea salt.
5. Serve.

Nutrition Information

Serving size: 2 pieces
Calories: 294
Total Fat: 14.8 g
Total Carbohydrate: 38.5 g
Sugars: 1.3 g
Protein: 9.7 g
Sodium: 419 mg

Roasted Eggplant Sandwich

Yield: 4 sandwiches

Ingredients

2 medium eggplants, cut into 1/2-inch rounds

4 tablespoons olive oil

Salt and pepper

3 tablespoons balsamic vinegar

1 baguette, cut into 4 pieces, each piece sliced in half

1 tablespoon plus 1 teaspoon olive oil

1/4 pound mozzarella

2 cups fresh basil leaves

Directions

1. If you have a Panini grill, preheat it to medium high.
2. Brush eggplant with oil and season with salt and pepper. Grill for 2-3 minutes, flip over and grill 3-4 minutes longer. Drizzle with balsamic vinegar.
3. Brush insides of baguette slices with oil. Layer basil, eggplant and cheese. Place

top slices and press in Panini press for 3
minutes for each side.

Nutrition Information

Serving size: 1 sandwich
Calories: 481
Total Fat: 23 g
Total Carbohydrate: 55 g
Sugars: 0.2 g
Protein: 26 g
Sodium:801

Veggie Fajitas

Yield: 8 fajitas

Ingredients

2 1/2 cups zucchini, julienne-cut

2 cups yellow squash, julienne-cut

2 cups red bell pepper strips

1 1/2 cups vertically sliced red onion

3 tablespoons vegetable soup and dip mix

4 teaspoons olive oil

8 (8-inch) flour tortillas, heated

1 (16-ounce) can fat-free refried beans, heated

2 cups leaf lettuce, shredded

1 cup reduced-fat cheddar cheese, shredded

1 cup tomato, chopped

1/2 cup salsa

Directions

1. Heat tortillas and refried beans according to package instructions.
2. Season zucchini, squash, bell peppers and onions with soup mix and oil. Mix well to coat evenly. Place in baking dish and bake at 450 degrees for 20 minutes. Stir, if needed.for even baking.
3. Layer each tortilla as follows:
   - 3 Tablespoons refried beans
   - 1/2 cup vegetable mixture
   - 1/4 cup lettuce
   - 2 Tablespoons cheese
   - 2 Tablespoons tomato
   - 1 Tablespoon salsa
4. Roll up and serve.

Nutrition Information

Serving size: 1 fajita
Calories: 309
Total Fat: 7.1 g
Total Carbohydrate: 48.6 g
Sugars: 3 g
Protein: 13.5 g
Sodium: 748 mg

Tomato Sandwiches

Yield: 2 sandwiches

Ingredients

2 Tablespoons ketchup

1 Tablespoon mayonnaise

 1/8 teaspoon salt

1/8 teaspoon hot pepper sauce

4 slices whole wheat bread

2 leaves lettuce

1 tomato, sliced

Directions

1. Combine first 4 ingredients. Mix well to make a sauce.
2. Toast bread.
3. Spread mayonnaise mixture over bread slices.
4. Layer lettuce followed by tomato on bread slice.
5. Top with second bread slice.
6. Repeat steps 3-5 for second sandwich.

Nutrition Information

Serving size: 2 sandwiches
Calories: 207
Total Fat: 7.6 g
Total Carbohydrate: 31.4 g
Sugars: 5.2 g
Protein: 5.4 g
Sodium: 628 mg

Focaccia with Basil and Pesto

Yield: 1 sandwich

Ingredients

1 slice focaccia bread, cut in half horizontally

1 Tablespoon mayonnaise

2 teaspoons basil pesto

2 Tablespoons sun-dried tomato pesto

1/4 cup red peppers, roasted

1/2 cup crumbled feta cheese

1/2 cup fresh basil leaves

Directions

1. Mix mayonnaise and pesto together to make a spread.
2. Spread over one slice of bread.
3. Spread the other slice with sun-dried tomato pesto. Place roasted peppers, followed by feta and finally fresh basil, on top.
4. Top with the other slice of bread.

Nutrition Information

Serving size: 1 sandwich
Calories: 720
Total Fat: 50.2 g
Total Carbohydrate: 40.6 g
Sugars: 8.1 g
Protein: 27 g
Sodium: 2127 mg

Cream Cheese and Veggies Spread

Yield: 15 servings

Ingredients

3 8-ounce packs cream cheese

6 green onions, sliced

1 large carrot, peeled, diced

1 stalk celery, finely diced

1/2 red bell pepper, finely diced

1/4 cup red onion, finely diced

1 Tablespoon chives, chopped

1 Tablespoon dill, chopped

1 clove garlic, peeled

Directions

1. Combine all ingredients in a food processor. Puree to desired consistency (whether chunky or smooth).
2. Chill.
3. Use as spread for bread and crackers.

Nutrition Information

Serving size: 1 (about 3 tablespoons)
Calories: 152
Total Fat: 14.8 g
Total Carbohydrate: 3.2 g
Sugars: 1.7 g
Protein: 3.5 g
Sodium: 133 mg

Nori Wraps

Yield: 3 wraps

Ingredients

3 nori seaweed sheets

1/2 cup hummus

1 1/2 Tablespoon hoisin sauce

1 cup fresh spinach

1/2 cup red cabbage, chopped finely

1/2 large carrot, peeled

1/2 avocado, pitted and sliced

small handful of cilantro, chopped

Directions

1. Lay nori on table, in landscape position.
2. The shiny side should be facing the table.
3. Spread hummus along edge closest to you.
4. On top of the hummus, layer each ingredient in desired amount (not too much or else nori will break).

5. Spread a very small amount of hummus on the other edge, to serve as "glue" to seal the roll.
6. Roll up away from you.
7. Slice diagonally and serve.

Nutrition Information

Serving size: 1.5 wraps
Calories: 258
Total Fat: 15.5 g
Total Carbohydrate: 23.7 g
Sugars: 1.7 g
Protein: 9.4 g
Sodium: 457 mg

The "Elvis" Sandwich

Yield: 1 sandwich

Ingredients

olive oil cooking spray

4 slices tempeh "bacon"

2 slices whole grain bread

3 Tablespoons peanut butter

1/2 medium banana, thinly sliced

Directions

1. Coat a skillet with olive oil cooking spray.
2. Over medium heat, brown tempeh bacon on both sides.
3. Spread both slices of bread with peanut butter.
4. Arrange banana slices on one bread slice, followed by tempeh bacon.
5. Cover with second bread slice.
6. Grill sandwich on a skillet over medium heat. Both sides should be golden brown.
7. Serve while hot.

Nutrition Information

Serving size: 1 sandwich
Calories: 409
Total Fat: 15.6 g
Total Carbohydrate: 48.5 g
Sugars: 10 g
Protein: 25 g
Sodium: 297 mg

Easy Pumpkin Butter

Yield: 4 1/2 cups (18 servings)

Ingredients

2 15-ounce cans pumpkin puree

2/3 cup coconut sugar (muscovado sugar or brown sugar may be substituted)

1/4 cup pure maple syrup

1/2 cup apple juice, unsweetened

1 Tablespoon lemon juice

2 1/2 teaspooons pumpkin pie spice

1/2 teaspoon ground cinnamon

pinch sea salt

Directions

1. Combine all ingredients in a pot and cook over medium heat.
2. Bring to a boil. When bubbling starts, reduce heat and simmer.
3. Simmer, while maintaining frequent bubbling, for at least 20 minutes.

4. Longer cooking time (5 -10 minutes longer) may be lengthened for thicker texture.
5. Allow to cool down.
6. Can be kept in the refrigerator for 2 weeks.
7. Serve with waffles, bread, crackers or pancakes.

Nutrition Information

Serving size: 1/4 cup
Calories: 59
Total Fat: 0.2 g
Total Carbohydrate:15 g
Sugars: 12.1 g
Protein: 0.5 g
Sodium: 15 mg

Mexican-Inspired Pita

Yield: 2 pita halves

Ingredients

1 whole wheat pita bread

1/2 cup vegetarian refried beans

3-4 thin slices of avocado

2 Tablespoons salsa

2 Tablespoons crumbled feta cheese, divided

hot sauce to taste

2 teaspoons fresh cilantro, chopped

Directions

1. Warm pita in oven or toaster oven until fragrant (1-2 minutes).
2. Cut in half.
3. Warm beans in a saucepan over medium heat. Heat through.
4. Turn off heat. While hot, add avocado. Mix.
5. Spoon bean mixture equally into the two pita slices.

6. Top with feta cheese, hot sauce and cilantro.

Nutrition Information

Serving size: 1 serving
Calories: 410
Total Fat: 14.1 g
Total Carbohydrate: 59.4 g
Sugars: 4.6 g
Protein: 16.5 g
Sodium: 1337 mg

Faux Tuna Spread

Yield: 4 servings

Ingredients

1 400-gram can chickpeas, drained and mashed

2 Tablespoons mayonnaise

2 teaspoons hot English mustard

1 Tablespoon sweet pickle relish

2 spring onions, chopped

Salt and pepper

Directions

1. Mix all ingredients together.
2. Use as sandwich filling.

Nutrition Information

Serving size: 1 serving
Calories: 170
Total Fat: 6.1 g
Total Carbohydrate: 23.3 g
Sugars: 0.5 g
Protein: 5.1 g
Sodium: 414 mg

SALAD RECIPES

Healthy Beet and Dill Salad

Yield: 6 servings

Ingredients

4 medium beetroots

1/3 cup sprouted fenugreek

1 teaspoon lemon juice

Salt and pepper to taste

1/4 cup chopped dill

1/4 cup chopped coriander

Directions

1. Boil the beets.
2. Peel the beets and cut into about 1-inch slices.
3. Mix with sprouted fenugreek, lemon juice, salt and pepper.
4. Let chill in refrigerator.
5. Add dill and coriander and toss just before serving.

Nutrition Information

Serving size: 1
Calories: 55
Total Fat: 0.6 g
Total Carbohydrate: 9.2 g
Sugars: 2.5 g
Protein: 3.3 g
Sodium: 50 mg

Farro Salad With Coco-Milk Dressing

Yield: 6 servings

Ingredients

For Dressing

1/2 cup light coconut milk

3 Tablespoons lime juice

2 Tablespoons shallot, finely chopped

1 Tablespoon olive oil

For salad

1 cup farro, uncooked

1/8 teaspoon salt

2 cups water

1 apple, cored and cut into 1/2-inch pieces

3 packed cups dinosaur kale, stems removed, leaves cut into 1-inch pieces

1/2 cup walnut halves, coarsely chopped

Salt and pepper to taste

Directions

<u>For dressing</u>

1. Whisk ingredients together in a bowl.
2. Set aside.

For salad

1. In a saucepan, mix farro, water and salt together. Boil for 6 minutes.

2. Reduce heat and simmer for about thirty minutes or until faro is tender and has absorbed the liquid.

3. Drain any excess liquid. Spread out the farro on a baking sheet or tray to cool. Season with more salt, if needed. Allow to cool for about 5 minutes.

4. Toss farro, apple and walnuts in a bowl.
5. Add dressing and toss. Season with salt and pepper, if needed.

Nutrition Information

Serving size: 1 serving
Calories: 231
Total Fat: 9 g
Total Carbohydrate: 33 g
Sugars: 4 g
Protein: 9 g
Sodium: 58 mg

Thai Salad

Yield: 4 servings

Ingredients

3 cups green papaya, shredded

Cold water

1/4 cup lime juice

1Tablespoon unsalted peanuts, crushed

5 cloves garlic, minced

2 teaspoon white miso paste

1 1/2 teaspoon light brown sugar

15 steamed green beans, cut into 1-inch pieces

1 Thai bird chili, thinly sliced

8 cherry tomatoes, halved

Topping

4 teaspoon green onion, thinly sliced

4 Tablespoons unsalted peanuts, crushed

Directions

1. Soak grated papaya in cold water for 10 minutes.
2. While papaya is soaking, place lime juice, 1 Tablespoon peanuts, garlic, miso and sugar in a blender. Blend into a puree.
3. Drain water from papaya.
4. Combine pureed peanut mixture with papaya, green beans and chili.
5. Gently mix in tomatoes.
6. Serve topped with crushed peanuts and chopped green onion.

Nutrition Information

Serving size: 1
Calories: 129
Total Fat: 6 g
Total Carbohydrate: 17 g
Sugars: 8 g
Protein: 4 g
Sodium: 92 mg

Greek Salad

Yield: 4 servings

Ingredients

3 Tablespoons olive oil

2 Tablespoons red wine vinegar

1/2 teaspoon sugar

1/4 teaspoon dried oregano

1 medium onion, halved and thinly sliced

2 cups romaine lettuce, chopped

2 medium cucumbers, peeled, cut into 1/2-inch slices

2 tomatoes, cut into wedges

1/2 cup reduced-fat feta cheese, crumbled

1/4 cup kalamata olives, optional

Salt and pepper

Directions

1. Make a vinaigrette by combining olive oil, red wine vinegar, sugar and oregano. Add sliced onion to vinaigrette, cover, and soak for at least 4 hours.
2. When vinaigrette is ready, toss together the rest of the ingredients. Add the vinaigrette. Season with salt and pepper, if needed.

Nutrition Information

Serving size: 1 1/2 cup serving
Calories: 162
Total Fat: 3 g
Total Carbohydrate: 8 g
Sugars: 4 g
Protein: 5 g
Sodium: 243 mg

Party Salad with Croutons

Yield: 8 servings

Ingredients

1/4 cup white balsamic vinegar

1/3 cup olive oil

1 small shallot, peeled and finely chopped

Salt and pepper

1 8-oz. loaf French bread

2 Tablespoons olive oil

1 large head radicchio, sliced into thin ribbons

3 cups Tuscan kale, ribs removed, leaves sliced into thin ribbons

2 white Belgian endives, sliced into thin rings

4 large dates, pitted and sliced into thin slivers

Directions

1. Make a vinaigrette by whisking balsamic vinegar and 1/3 cup olive oil together. Add shallots and season with salt and pepper.
2. For croutons, preheat oven to 350 degrees. Remove crust from bread and discard. Tear bread into ½-inch pieces. In a bowl, toss bread pieces with 2 Tablespoons olive oil. Transfer the oiled bread pieces to a baking sheet. Spread out and bake for about 20 minutes. Stir to ensure even browning. Croutons are done when golden brown.
3. Put 6 Tablespoons of the vinaigrette in a bowl. Add radicchio and kale and toss. Massage greens gently to wilt.
4. Add other ingredients and toss.
5. Serve with vinaigrette on the side.

Nutrition Information

Serving size: 1 1/4 cups
Calories: 221
Total Fat: 13 g
Total Carbohydrate: 24 g
Sugars: 6 g
Protein: 5 g
Sodium: 147 mg

Salad Greens with Rhubarb, Pecan and Goat Cheese

Yield: 4 servings

Ingredients

3 ribs rhubarb, cut into ½-inch chunks

2 Tablespoons sugar

1/3 cup pecans, coarsely chopped

2 Tablespoons balsamic vinegar

1Tablespoons olive oil

1 shallot, finely chopped

4 cups mixed greens

1/2 cup goat cheese

Directions

1. To prepare rhubarb, preheat oven to 450 degrees. Mix rhubarb with sugar. Spread on baking sheet and bake for about 5 minutes or until rhubarb softens.
2. Heat a skillet over medium heat and cook pecans for 3-4 minutes to toast.
3. In a salad bowl, whisk vinegar with oil. Toss in shallots and mixed greens.
4. Serve topped with rhubarb, pecans and goat cheese.

Nutrition Information

Serving size: 1 1/2 cups
Calories: 182
Total Fat: 13 g
Total Carbohydrate: 13 g
Sugars: 9 g
Protein: 4 g
Sodium: 89 mg

Fingerling Potato Salad

Ingredients

8 cups fingerling potatoes, cut into 1-inch pieces

1/2 cup plain low-fat yogurt

1/4 cup whole-grain mustard

2 teaspoons olive oil

1 small red bell pepper, diced

3 celery stalks, diced

1/2 small red onion, sliced

Directions

1. Cook potatoes in a saucepan, covered with water. Boil for about 5 minutes or until potatoes are tender (not too soft). Drain the potatoes and rinse twice with cold water. Drain again.
2. In a bowl, combine yogurt, mustard and olive oil. Stir.
3. Stir in bell pepper, celery, onion, and potatoes. Season with salt and pepper.

Nutrition Information

Serving size: 1 cup
Calories: 134
Total Fat: 2 g
Total Carbohydrate: 24 g
Sugars: 3 g
Protein: 4 g
Sodium: 182 mg

Fruit and Chili Salad

Yield: 6 servings

Ingredients

1 small lime, juiced

1 Tablespoon maple or agave syrup

1/4 teaspoon chili powder

Sea salt

2 ripe mangos, peeled and cubed

4 kiwi, peeled and sliced

1 cup strawberries, sliced

1 cup blueberries

1 ounce tequila or white rum (optional)

Directions

1. Whisk together lime juice, syrup, chili and salt.
2. Place fruits in a large bowl. Pour chili mixture over the fruit, gently tossing to distribute flavor. Adjust seasonings according to taste.
3. Add tequila or white rum (optional).

Nutrition Information

Serving size: 1 cup
Calories: 112
Total Fat: 0.7 g
Total Carbohydrate: 27.4 g
Sugars: 20.6 g
Protein: 1.3 g
Sodium: 44 mg

Tropical Fruits With Vegan Cashew Cream

Yield: 3-4 servings

Ingredients

<u>For cashew cream</u>

    3/4 cup cashews

    1 teaspoon vanilla extract

    Sugar, as required

    Chilled water

<u>For fruit salad</u>

    1 cup pineapple, chopped

    1 cup apple, peeled, cored and chopped

    1 cup banana, chopped

    1 cup musk melon, chopped

    1 cup papaya, chopped

    1 cup any other tropical fruit (mango, sapodilla, watermelon, etc.)

    Pistachios, chopped (optional)

Directions

<u>For cashew cream</u>

1. Rinse cashew nuts. Drain.
2. Put in a bowl or container. Add water just to cover the nuts.
3. Cover and let soak. Refrigerate for 5 hours.
4. Drain off water and place cashew nuts in a blender.
5. Pour chilled water into the blender. It should be just enough to cover the nuts. More water may be added later for a thinner cream. Add vanilla and sugar (optional). Other sweeteners may be used, as desired. Blend until smooth. Adjust thickness (with water) or sweetness, if needed. Keep chilled.

<u>Assembling the salad</u>

1. Mix the fruits together in a bowl. Serve topped with cashew cream and pistachios (optional).
2. Variation: Layer fruit and cream by in wine goblets and top with pistachios.

Nutrition Information

Serving size: 1 1/2 cups
Calories: 278
Total Fat: 12.5 g
Total Carbohydrate: 34.8 g
Sugars: 16.2 g
Protein: 5.1 g
Sodium: 20 mg

Spinach and "Bacon" Salad

Yield: 4 servings

Ingredients

1/2 cup vegetable oil

3 medium cloves garlic, halved lengthwise

1 teaspoon dried oregano

1 Tablespoon peanut oil

1/2 cup tempeh, chopped

3 Tablespoons red wine vinegar

1 teaspoon fresh lemon juice

1/4 teaspoon salt

1/4 teaspoon black pepper

8 cups fresh spinach, stemmed, rinsed well, dried and coarsely torn

4 thinly sliced onion rings

2 large button mushrooms, thinly sliced

1 large scallion, thinly sliced

Directions

1. Place oil and garlic in a saucepan and heat until oil bubbles gently. When garlic is tender (no browned yet), add oregano. Remove from heat. Allow to stand for 30 minutes for flavors to infuse into the oil.
2. Remove the cooked garlic from the oil and mince into a paste.
3. In a skillet, warm the peanut oil and cook the tempeh over medium heat. Cook, with some mixing, for about 8 minutes or until crisp. Transfer tempeh to a plate or bowl.
4. In the warm skillet with peanut oil, add 2 Tablespoons of the previously flavored oil, and the garlic paste. Add vinegar, lemon juice, salt and pepper. Heat to a simmer.
5. Place spinach, onion rings, mushrooms and scallions in a heat-resistant serving bowl. Pour newly-simmered oil on top.
6. Sprinkle with crispy tempeh and serve. Note: Remaining garlic- and oregano-flavored oil may still be used in later recipes for salads or for flavoring other dishes.

Nutrition Information

Serving size: 1 serving
Calories: 170
Total Fat: 12 g
Total Carbohydrate: 9 g
Sugars: 0.6 g
Protein: 7 g
Sodium: 181 mg

TOFU RECIPES

Why eat tofu?

Tofu, or bean curd, is a great ingredient for vegetarian and vegan dishes. It has a somewhat neutral flavor that makes it a versatile ingredient for many dishes. It can be fried, boiled, steamed, baked, grilled or used uncooked; lending different textures to a variety of dishes.

Tofu is the result of curdling soybean milk. It is made from white soybeans that are boiled and strained. The strained milk is then curdled like cheese. There are different textures like firm, soft and silken. There are also different kinds like custard tofu and smoked tofu.

The protein in soybeans is called a *complete* protein because it contains all eight essential amino acids. This is what makes soybeans stand out among other vegetable sources of protein. Amino acids in almost all other plant sources are incomplete. Soybeans are also a good source of iron, calcium, B vitamins, and fiber. Soybeans and soybean products contain vitamin B_{12}, which is usually only found more abundantly in meat, dairy, seafood and eggs. Substances found in soybeans are said to help lower cholesterol, prevent cancer, reduce the risks of developing type 2 diabetes and even relieve the symptoms of menopause. Soy products also help prevent bone degeneration and obesity. Soy products like tofu should therefore be a part of one's diet. In this section, you'll find delicious and easy-to-prepare dishes full of the healthful goodness of tofu.

The Secrets to Great-Tasting Tofu Dishes

There's a little secret to making tofu taste its best in any dish: you need to "press" it before cooking. This means putting a weight on it to squeeze out the liquid. It helps improve texture and absorption of flavors from marinades, spices and sauces. Here's how to do it:

1. Take the tofu out of its packaging and put it on a plate.
2. Put another plate on top of the tofu and weigh it down with something that weighs about 1 pound, like a can of corn.
3. After 30 minutes, pour out any squeezed-out liquid.
4. The tofu may be cooked at this point or you can repeat the process and extend pressing to 2-3 hours to squeeze out as much liquid as possible. For longer pressing time (overnight, for example), wrap the tofu in towels before placing weight and keep refrigerated.
   Note: Pressing of tofu is best for most recipes except for those that make use of uncooked silken tofu like Tofu Smoothie and Tofu Tiramisu.

Now that you know the secret, you're sure to get delicious results!

Scrambled "Eggs"

Yield: 12 muffins

Ingredients

200 grams extra firm tofu

1 Tablespoon onion powder

1/2 teaspoon turmeric powder

2 Tablespoon soy sauce

Salt and pepper

2 teaspoons olive oil

1 teaspoon garlic, minced

1/2 red bell pepper, diced

Directions

1. After pressing the tofu for 20-30 minutes, place in a bowl. Crumble the tofu to make it look like scrambled egg whites.
2. Season with onion powder, turmeric, soy sauce, salt and pepper. Mix well.
3. Heat a non-stick frying pan or skillet over medium heat. Add olive oil and sauté garlic and red pepper for 5-10 minutes.

4. Put in the scrambled tofu mixture. Continue cooking for about 10 more minutes, making sure all the ingredients are evenly coated with seasoning and tofu is evenly yellowed.
5. Serve immediately.

Nutrition Information

Serving size: 2
Calories: 371
Total Fat: 19 g
Total Carbohydrate: 38 g
Sugars: 23 g
Protein: 16 g
Sodium: 1500 mg

Hot and Sour Soup

Yield: 3 1/2 servings

Ingredients

6 cups vegetable broth

4 fresh shiitake mushrooms, cleaned and sliced

1/2 cup water chestnuts

5 Tablespoons rice wine vinegar

4 Tablespoons soy sauce

1/2 cup bamboo shoots, drained and sliced

1 teaspoon hot sauce

1/4 teaspoon hot pepper flakes

1 cup firm tofu, cut in cubes

1 egg

5 green onions, finely chopped

Optional:

For slurry (thickener)

2 Tablespoons flour

1/2 cup cool water

Directions

1. In a pot, bring vegetable broth to a boil.
2. Add ingredients except tofu, egg and green onions. Reduce heat and simmer for about 20 minutes. Soup may be thickened, if desired, with a slurry of flour mixed in water (add 1/2 cup cool water to 2 Tablespoons flour, mix and whisk into the broth).
3. While simmering the broth, whisk the egg in a small bowl.
4. Stir the soup to make a "whirlpool" in its center. Slowly pour in the beaten egg, while swirling, to make ribbons.
5. Add the tofu cubes and cook through for about 1 minute.
6. Remove from heat.
7. Serve garnished with chopped green onion.

Nutrition Information

Serving size: 2 cups
Calories: 180
Total Fat: 5.1 g
Total Carbohydrate: 19.6 g
Sugars: 3.5 g
Protein: 13.6 g
Sodium: 1263 mg

Tofu Tacos

Yield: 8 tacos

Ingredients

1 package extra-firm tofu, drained

1/4 cup whole wheat flour

1/4 cup nutritional yeast

2 teaspoons onion powder

1/2 teaspoon garlic powder

1/4 teaspoon turmeric

2 Tablespoons liquid aminos

8 corn tortillas, warmed

Salsa

Suggested toppings: avocado, cilantro, bell peppers, onions, lettuce, tomatoes, etc.

Directions

1. Crumble pressed tofu in a bowl and add flour, yeast, onion powder, garlic powder and turmeric. Toss to coat evenly. Add aminos and toss again.

2. Cook the tofu mixture in a heated skillet. Use medium heat. Stir frequently to prevent sticking. Some parts should be brown and crisp.
3. Serve with tortillas and toppings.

Nutrition Information

Serving size: 1 taco
Calories: 250
Total Fat: 7 g
Total Carbohydrate: 31 g
Sugars: 1 g
Protein: 17 g
Sodium: 570 mg

Tofu "Huevos Rancheros"

Yield: 6 servings

Ingredients

2 14-ounce blocks extra-firm tofu

2 tablespoons vegetable oil

1 small onion, chopped

1 small green bell pepper, finely chopped

1 small red bell pepper, finely chopped

1/2 teaspoon ground coriander

1/2 teaspoon ground cumin

1 1/2 teaspoons ground turmeric

1 15-ounce can black beans, rinsed, drained

1/4 cup coarsely chopped fresh cilantro

Salt and pepper

6 whole wheat tortillas, warmed

Toppings and Garnishes: sliced scallions, grated cheese, salsa, avocado, etc. ,

Directions

1. After pressing the tofu, mash in a bowl with a fork.
2. Put oil in a skillet over medium heat. Sauté onions and peppers until tender. Add coriander and cumin. Cook, with stirring, until fragrant. Stir in mashed tofu and turmeric. Mix to distribute the yellow color on the tofu. Add beans and cook to heat through, with constant stirring.
3. Season with salt and pepper.
4. Serve with tortillas and suggested toppings.

Nutrition Information

Serving size: 1 serving
Calories: 390
Total Fat: 16 g
Total Carbohydrate: 43 g
Sugars: 5 g
Protein: 22 g
Sodium: 620 mg

Tofu Skewers

Yield: 4 servings

Ingredients

8 button onions

3 cups boiling water

8 small new potatoes

2 Tablespoons tomato purée

2 Tablespoons light soy sauce

1 Tablespoon sunflower oil

1 Tablespoon clear honey

1 Tablespoon wholegrain mustard

2 3/4 cups firm smoked tofu, cubed

1 zucchini, peeled and sliced

1 red pepper, deseeded and diced

Directions

1. Put the button onions in a bowl and cover with boiling water. Let stand for 5 minutes.

2. Cook potatoes in boiling water until tender (about 7 minutes). Drain and allow to dry.
3. In a bowl, make a marinade of tomato puree, soy sauce, oil, honey, mustard, salt and pepper. Toss in the tofu. Allow to soak for at least 10 minutes.
4. Drain button onions and peel. Cook in boiling water for 3 minutes and drain.
5. Heat the grill.
6. Assemble the skewers by threading tofu, onion, potato, zucchini and pepper through.
7. Grill, turning frequently and brushing with marinade. Tofu skewers should be done after about 10 minutes of grilling.

Nutrition Information

Serving size: 1
Calories: 178
Total Fat: 8 g
Total Carbohydrate: 18 g
Sugars: 3 g
Protein: 10 g
Sodium: 3470 mg

Tofu Smoothie

Yield: 2 servings

Ingredients

1/2 cup silken tofu

1 ripe banana

2 cups frozen mixed berries

1/2 cup fresh orange juice

Directions

Put all ingredients together in a blender. Blend until smooth.

Nutrition Information

Serving size: 1 serving
Calories: 182
Total Fat: 1.9 g
Total Carbohydrate: 38.6 g
Sugars: 18 g
Protein: 4.8 g
Sodium: 42 mg

Ginger and Bok Choy Tofu

Yield: 2 servings

Ingredients

1 cup firm tofu, pressed well and drained

2 tbsp peanut oil, divided

1 thumb ginger, sliced

1/2 cup bok choy, leaves separated

1 Tablespoon rice wine

1 Tablespoon rice vinegar

1/2 teaspoon dried chili flakes

For the marinade:

1 Tablespoon grated ginger

1 teaspoon dark soy sauce

2 Tablespoons light soy sauce

1 Tablespoon brown sugar

Directions

1. For best results, press tofu for a longer period of time for more liquid to be squeezed out and for better absorption of marinade. After pressing, drain tofu and cut into 1-inch pieces.
2. Combine marinade ingredients in a bowl. Marinate tofu for 15 minutes.
3. Heat a wok or frying pan. Add 1 Tablespoon peanut oil and heat almost to smoking. Add the ginger and heat until fragrant. Add the bok choy. Stir-fry for a 2 minutes. Add about 1/8 cup water and cook about 2 minutes longer. Bok choy leaves should be wilted but stems should still be a little crisp. Season with salt and pepper. Transfer to serving dish.
4. Remove tofu from marinade. Set aside remaining marinade.
5. In another wok, heat the rest of the peanut oil to almost smoking point. Add tofu and stir-fry until evenly browned. Add a little more oil, if needed. Add remaining marinade, rice wine and vinegar. Sauce should start to bubble. Allow to reduce and thicken a little. Sprinkle with chili flakes and spoon over bok choy in serving dish.
6. Serve with rice.

Nutrition Information

Serving size: 1
Calories: 241
Total Fat: 15 g
Total Carbohydrate:16 g
Sugars: 11 g
Protein: 11 g
Sodium: 347 mg

Macaroni and Tofu Salad

Yield: 8 servings

Ingredients

For the salad

1 15-ounce pack extra firm tofu, drained and pressed

1 1/2 Tablespoons sesame oil

1 8-ounce pack macaroni, pre-cooked according to packaging instructions

1/2 medium red onion, minced

3/4 bell pepper, chopped

3 cloves garlic, minced

For the dressing:

2 Tablespoons red wine vinegar

1 Tablespoon extra virgin olive oil

1 Tablespoon lemon juice

1/2 Tablespoon freshly grated lemon zest

1 1/2 teaspoons low-sodium soy sauce

Salt and pepper

1 teaspoon oregano

2 garlic cloves, crushed

For garnish

Fresh mozzarella slices (optional)

Mint sprigs for garnish

Directions

1. Cut tofu into bite-size pieces.
2. Heat about 2 1/2 teaspoons of the oil, in a skillet or non-stick pan, over high heat. Brown the tofu evenly (about 5 minutes). Set tofu aside. If possible, keep warm by placing in a warm oven.
3. Add remaining oil into skillet and cook onion, bell pepper and garlic until tender. Remove from heat and add macaroni and tofu. Mix well. Transfer to serving dish.
4. Prepare dressing by whisking all dressing ingredients together.
5. Pour dressing over macaroni.
6. Serve garnished with cheese and mint.

Nutrition Information

Serving size: 1 1/2 cups
Calories: 180
Total Fat: 6 g
Total Carbohydrate:24 g
Sugars: 1.1 g
Protein: 9 g
Sodium: 69 mg

Miso Soup

Yield: 4 servings

Ingredients

6 ounces tofu, cubed

3/4 cup fresh mushrooms, sliced

1 cup leafy vegetable, chopped

1 egg, whisked

2 Tablespoons green onion, chopped

4 cups vegetable broth

4 Tablespoons miso paste

Directions

1. Boil the broth in a pot. Add tofu, mushrooms and greens.
2. Stir the broth to create a "whirlpool" and slowly pour in egg. Cook for about 2 minutes more.
3. In a small bowl, mix miso paste and bout 1/2 cup of hot broth. When miso has dissolved, pour into the pot. Stir..
4. Serve topped with green onion.

Nutrition Information

Serving size: 1 serving
Calories: 76
Total Fat: 3.3 g
Total Carbohydrate: 5.6 g
Sugars: 4.2 g
Protein: 6.2 g
Sodium: 637 mg

Sweet Potato and Mustard-Crusted Tofu

Yield: 4 servings

Ingredients

1 14-ounce package firm tofu,pressed, cut into 1/2-inch slices

1/2 cup whole grain Dijon mustard

4 Tablespoons vegetable oil, divided

1/2 medium onion, sliced

1 Tablespoon fresh ginger, peeled and minced

8 cups kale, stem cut from each leaf, leaves thinly sliced crosswise

1 small red-skinned sweet potato, peeled, halved lengthwise, thinly sliced crosswise

2 Tablespoons fresh lime juice

Directions

1. Make sure the tofu slices have been well drained and dried. Pat dry with towels, if needed. Coat evenly with mustard.
2. In a non-stick skillet, heat 2 Tablespoons of the oil over medium heat. Sauté onion

and ginger until fragrant. Add the last 3 ingredients. Reduce heat, cover, and cook for about 12 minutes or until sweet potatoes are tender.

3. In another skillet, heat the remaining oil over medium heat and add the tofu slices. Cover and cook for about 2 minutes on each side or until surface is crisp.

4. Transfer potato and kale on a serving dish and arrange tofu on top.

Nutrition Information

Serving size: 1
Calories: 418
Total Fat: 24 g
Total Carbohydrate: 31 g
Sugars: 4.0
Protein: 21 g
Sodium: 775 mg

Tasty Tofu Stir-Fry

Yield: 2 servings

Ingredients

For the Stir Fry

1 14-ounce package firm tofu, pressed well, cut into 1-inch cubes

2 cups green beans, chopped

1/2 cup carrots, diced

1/2 cup red pepper, diced

2 Tablespoons sesame oil

For the Sauce

1/4 cup soy sauce, low-sodium, gluten free

1 Tablespoon fresh ginger, grated

2 Tablespoons brown sugar

1 Tablespoon syrup of choice (agave, maple, or honey if not vegan)

1 Tablespoon corn starch

Directions

1. Preheat oven to 400 degrees. Line a baking sheet with parchment paper or coat lightly with non-stick cooking spray.
2. Pat tofu dry with towels and arrange on baking sheet. Bake for about 20 minutes, checking now and then and flipping, to prevent sticking and to ensure cooking is even. Baking may be extended 5-10 minutes longer if a more meat-like texture is desired. Remove from heat when golden brown.
3. Prepare sauce by whisking all its ingredients in a bowl. Set aside.
4. Heat the sesame oil in a large skillet over medium heat. Stir-fry veggies for about 5 minutes or until the veggies are tender-crisp. Add the sauce and stir. When sauce bubbles and thickens, add the tofu. Heat may be reduced to prevent scorching. Stir tofu to coat with sauce. Let simmer, with constant stirring, for 3-5 minutes.
5. Serve with rice.

Nutrition Information

Serving size: 2
Calories: 371
Total Fat: 19 g
Total Carbohydrate: 38 g
Sugars: 23 g
Protein: 16 g
Sodium: 1500 mg

Tofu Stir-Fry With Eggplant

Yield: 4 servings

Ingredients

4 Tablespoons canola oil, divided

1 pound firm tofu, pressed, drained, patted dry, and cut into 1-inch cubes

1 small eggplant, cut into 1/2-inch pieces

4 scallions, sliced, white and green parts separated

2 cloves garlic, chopped

1 red serrano or jalapeño chili, sliced

Salt to taste

1/4cup fresh basil leaves, torn

For sauce

1/2 cup hoisin sauce

3 Tablespoons rice vinegar

1 teaspoon cornstarch

Directions

1. In a small bowl, whisk together sauce ingredients and set aside.
2. Heat 1Tablespoon oil in a skillet over medium heat. Brown the tofu in the oil, stirring for about 8 minutes. Transfer to a bowl of plate.
3. Add the remaining oil to the skillet and cook eggplant, scallion whites, garlic, chili and salt.Toss for about 8-10 minutes or until eggplant is tender and slightly browned.
4. Add the sauce mixture, tofu and scallion greens. Stir gently and continuously for about 2 minutes or until sauce has thickened.
5. Garnish with basil and serve with rice.

Nutrition Information

Serving size: 1
Calories: 523
Total Fat: 20 g
Total Carbohydrate:67 g
Sugars: 12 g
Protein: 17 g
Sodium: 644 mg

Tofu Burger

Yield: 4 servings

Ingredients

1 14-ounce extra-firm tofu, pressed, drained

2 Tablespoons olive oil

4 slices cheddar cheese

1 4-ounce package alfalfa sprouts

1 small bunch radishes, sliced

4 whole-wheat rolls, toasted

Honey mustard (optional)

For marinade

1/2 cup soy sauce

2 Tablespoons brown sugar

1 Tablespoon white vinegar

Directions

1. Cut the well-pressed tofu into 1-inch thick slices. Pat dry with a towel.
2. Prepare the marinade by cooking ingredients in a saucepan over medium heat. Cook with constant stirring until thickened (about 5-7 minutes).
3. Pour marinade over tofu and let stand for 15 minutes. Flip over midway.
4. Heat oil in a grill pan at medium heat. Grill the patties for about 2 minutes on each side.
5. Top tofu with cheese and grill further to melt cheese. Top further with sprouts and radishes to heat through.
6. Serve in rolls with mustard dressing (optional).

Nutrition Information

Serving size: 1 burger
Calories: 321
Total Fat: 17 g
Total Carbohydrate: 24 g
Sugars: 6 g
Protein: 22 mg
Sodium: 862 g

Stuffed Tofu

Yield: 4 servings

Ingredients

1 20-ounce pack baked, marinated tofu

3 teaspoons olive oil

1 ½ tsp. curry powder

1 small clove garlic, minced

1 teaspoon fresh ginger, minced

6 scallions (white and light green parts), thinly sliced

1/2 small red bell pepper, finely chopped

1/2 small green bell pepper, finely chopped

1 teaspoon tamari or soy sauce

1/4 cup chopped fresh cilantro, plus additional for garnish

For sauce

1 Tablespoon soy sauce

1 Tablespoon rice vinegar

1 Tablespoon. mirin

1 1/2 teaspoon scallion tops, minced

1 teaspoon dark sesame oil

Directions

1. If not pre-sliced, cut tofu into 4 equal slices.
2. Prepare the dipping sauce by whisking the sauce ingredients in a bowl. Set aside to allow flavors to meld.
3. Heat 2 teaspoons olive oil in a large skillet over medium heat. Stir in curry powder. Add tofu slices, cooking about 2 minutes per side or until golden brown. Transfer to dish lined with paper towels.
4. Keep skillet warm and remove any stuck bits. Add the remaining olive oil. Add garlic and cook until fragrant. Follow with ginger and cook also until fragrant (about 30 seconds). Add the vegetables, except cilantro, and cook for about 3 minutes or until tender. Remove from heat. Stir in cilantro.
5. Slit tofu horizontally about three-quarters through. Transfer to serving dish. Stuff each with vegetable mixture. Sprinkle with additional cilantro (optional) and serve with dipping sauce.

Nutrition Information

Serving size: 1
Calories: 95
Total Fat: 7 g
Total Carbohydrate: 4 g
Sugars: 2.5 g
Protein: 6 g
Sodium: 346 mg

Tofu Tiramisu

Yield: 8 servings

Ingredients

2 14-ounce packs silken tofu

1 1/2 cups margarine

5 Tablespoons sugar

5 Tablespoons orange juice

3 Tablespoons amaretto syrup

1 14-ounce pack lady finger cookies

1 1/2 cups coffee or espresso, cold

4 Tablespoons cocoa powder

Directions

1. Soften margarine in a double boiler or over low heat.
2. In a blender, combine silken tofu, orange juice, sugar and amaretto syrup. Blend into a puree. Stir in the margarine and stir or blend further until well-incorporated. This will serve as the cream layer.
3. Prepare the lady finger cookies by dipping each in the coffee.
4. Line serving dish with lady fingers. Follow with a layer of cream.

5. Repeat, ending with cream layer.
6. Sift cocoa powder over top (this may be done just before serving, if desired).
7. Refrigerate overnight or for at least 3 hours.

Nutrition Information

Serving size: 1 serving
Calories: 590
Total Fat: 40.8
Total Carbohydrate: 48.45
Sugars: 27.5
Protein: 9.3
Sodium: 614 mg

STUFFED AND BAKED RECIPES

Cranberry and Spinach Stuffed Sweet Potatoes

Yield: 3 servings

Ingredients

3 medium sweet potatoes, washed and dried

2 Tablespoons vegetable oil, divided

1 clove garlic, minced

3 cups fresh spinach, stems removed

1 1/2 Tablespoons butter

1/3 cup walnuts, chopped

3 Tablespoon dried cranberries

Salt & pepper

Directions

1. Preheat oven to 400 degrees.
2. Prick sweet potatoes with a fork and rub with 1 Tablespoon oil.
3. Bake for about 45 minutes to 1 hour or until potatoes are soft at their centers when pricked with a fork.

4. While baking potatoes, heat 1 Tablespoon oil in a skillet over medium heat. Cook garlic until fragrant. Add spinach, season with salt and pepper, and cook for 2-3 minutes or until wilted. Remove from heat.
5. Transfer potatoes to dishes, slice open in the middle and mash slightly with a fork.
6. Place 1/2 teaspoon butter on each open potato and season with salt and pepper.
7. Spoon spinach mixture over potatoes. Top with walnuts and cranberries, and serve.

Nutrition Information

Serving size: 1 serving
Calories: 335
Total Fat: 20.8 g
Total Carbohydrate: 35.4 g
Sugars: 0.7 g
Protein: 5.0 g
Sodium: 139 mg

Stuffed Eggplant with Basil and Mozzarella

Yield: 4 servings

Ingredients

2 medium eggplants, halved lengthwise, stems intact

2 Tablespoons olive oil

1 large onion, finely chopped

4 garlic cloves, finely chopped

12 cherry tomatoes, halved

1/4 cup pitted green olives, chopped

1 cupl basil leaves, chopped

1 cup vegetarian mozzarella, torn into bite-size pieces

1/2 cup fresh white breadcrumbs

Salt and pepper

Directions

1. Preheat oven to 400 degrees.

2. Prepare the eggplants by scooping out the flesh, leaving about 0.5-1 cm from skin intact. Chop flesh and set aside.

3. Brush eggplants with about a teaspoon of oil and season with salt and pepper. Wrap in foil and bake for 20 minutes or until tender.

4. In a skillet, add remaining oil. Cook onions over medium heat still soft. Stir in chopped eggplant flesh and cook through. Add garlic and tomatoes and cook for 3 more minutes. Stir in olives, basil, mozzarella and seasoning. Remove from heat.

5. Take eggplant shells out of oven. Reduce oven heat to 350 degrees.

6. Spoon filling into the baked eggplant shells. Sprinkle with crumbs and drizzle with a little oil. Bake for 15-20 minutes or until breadcrumbs are golden brown.

Nutrition Information

Serving size : 1 serving
Calories: 266
Total Fat: 20 g
Total Carbohydrate: 14 g
Sugars: 7 g
Protein: 9 g
Sodium: 1170 mg

Quinoa-Stuffed Peppers with Avocado Cream

Yield: 4 servings

Ingredients

For the stuffed peppers:

Cooking spray

1/2 cup cashews, soaked in very hot water

4 large bell peppers

1 8-ounce jar red enchilada sauce

2 cups frozen spinach, thawed with water squeezed out

1 heaping cup cooked quinoa

1 15-ounce can black beans, drained and rinsed

1/2 medium sweet potato, grated

1/2 cup chunky salsa

1/2 cup corn

1/2 teaspoon salt

1/2 teaspoon garlic powder

1/2 teaspoon cumin powder

1/4 teaspoon cayenne powder

For the avocado cream:

1 avocado

Juice 1 lime

1/2 teaspoon salt

1/4 cup almond, milk unsweetened, unflavored

Directions

1. Preheat oven to 375 degrees. Prepare a baking dish or sheet by coating with cooking spray.
2. Carefully cut off tops of peppers. Remove stems from tops and chop. Set aside 1/2 cup of chopped pepper tops.
3. Gently clean out insides of peppers, removing white parts. Place in baking dish, cut side up, and bake for 15 minutes. Remove from heat and set aside.
4. Drain the soaked cashews. In a blender, combine cashews, enchilada sauce and 1/2 cup chopped peppers. Blend until smooth.
5. In a large bowl, combine the rest of the ingredients (except those for the avocado

cream). Stir. Add cashew enchilada sauce and mix well.

6. Spoon mixture into bell peppers shells and bake for 25 minutes.

7. While baking stuffed peppers, prepare avocado cream. Place the avocado cream ingredients in a blender. Blend until smooth.

8. Serve stuffed peppers drizzled with avocado cream.

Nutrition Information

Serving size: 1 serving
Calories: 517
Total Fat: 19.5 g
Total Carbohydrate: 72.2 g
Sugars: 7 g
Protein: 20.6 g
Sodium: 1,389 mg

Festive Seitan Loaf with Vegetable Stuffing

Yield: 10 servings

Ingredients

Stuffing:

2 cups butternut squash,peeled and cubed

1 tablespoon olive oil

1/2 onion, chopped

1 stalk celery, chopped

1 carrot, chopped

1/2 cup mushrooms, chopped

2 cloves garlic, minced

1 cup kale, chopped

1/4 cup dried cranberries

1 teaspoon oregano

1 teaspoon dried thyme

2 Tablespoons bread crumbs

Salt and pepper

Seitan Roast:

2 cups vital wheat gluten

1/3 cup garbanzo bean flour

2 cups vegetable broth

1 teaspoon garlic powder

1 teaspoon onion powder

1 teaspoon dried oregano

1 teaspoon celery salt

1/4 teaspoon dried rosemary

Gravy:

16 ounces mushrooms, chopped

4 Tablespoons olive oil

2 cloves garlic, minced

4 Tablespoons flour

4 cups vegetable broth

2 Tablespoons fresh oregano, chopped

Salt and pepper

Directions

For stuffing

1. Preheat oven to 350 degrees.
2. Add olive oil to squash cubes and toss. Bake until tender (about 1 hour). Set aside.
3. Heat 1 Tablespoon oil in a skillet over medium heat. Cook onion, celery and carrot until tender. Add mushrooms and cook 2 minutes more. Add kale and garlic and continue cooking until kale is wilted.
4. Toss in squash, cranberries, oregano and thyme. After 1 minute, remove from heat and stir in breadcrumbs. Season with salt and pepper.
5. Transfer to a food processor and pulse 10-12 times just until stuffing starts to stick together. Set aside.

To make the seitan roast

1. Preheat oven to 350 degrees.
2. In a large mixing bowl, combine seitan ingredients. Mix until it forms a ball of dough.
3. Prepare a piece of aluminum foil, about 2 feet long. Spray with cooking oil.

4. Place the dough on the center of the foil and use your hands to spread the dough into a rectangle, roughly 10-inch x 12-inch.

5. Spoon 2 cups of the stuffing onto the center of the dough. Leave about 2 inches of space at the ends. Grabbing the foil, bring the longer sides of the seitan up and over the filling. Pinch the ends of the dough to seal. Fold the aluminum foil over the dough tightly.

6. Place on a baking sheet and bake for 1 hour. Every 25 minutes, roll the loaf a quarter turn.

7. After baking, allow to cool and then peel off the aluminum foil.

To make the gravy

1. In a large skillet, heat olive oil over medium heat. Add mushrooms and cook until the liquid from the mushrooms is reduced (about 7 minutes). Toss in garlic and flour. Make sure to coat the mushrooms.

2. Add vegetable broth and stir well. Simmer for about 10-12 minutes or until gravy has thickened.

Serve sliced the seitan roast (1-inch to 1 1/2-inch slices), topped with gravy.

Nutrition Information

Serving size: 1 slice
Calories: 190
Total Fat: 7.7 g
Total Carbohydrate: 18.1 g
Sugars: 3.4 g
Protein: 13.4 g
Sodium:645 mg

Stuffed Avocado

Yield: 1 serving

Ingredients

1/4 cup fresh breadcrumbs

2 Tablespoons Red Leicester cheese, grated (or cheddar cheese)

1 medium avocado

1 Tablespoon olive oil

1/4 small onion, chopped

1 ounce pine kernels

Salt and pepper to taste

Directions

1. Combine breadcrumbs and cheese. Set aside.
2. Scoop flesh out of avocado, leaving a small allowance on skin. Chop avocado flesh and set aside.
3. Preheat oven to 350 degrees.
4. Heat oil in a skillet over medium heat. Cook the onion until tender then add the avocado. Cook for about 1 minute and then add pine kernels. Cook for about 2 minutes or until kernels are somewhat

toasted. Remove from heat. Season with salt and pepper.

5. Spoon the filling into avocado shells. Top with cheese and breadcrumb mixture.

6. Bake for about 30 minutes or until

breadcrumbs are golden brown.

Nutrition Information

Serving size: 1 serving
Calories: 634
Total Fat: 58.7 g
Total Carbohydrate: 28.1 g
Sugars: 8 g
Protein: 10 g
Sodium: 302 mg

Stuffed Mushrooms

Yield: 14 mushrooms

Ingredients

1/2 cup black rice, rinsed

1 cup vegetable stock

1 10-ounce package baby Portobello mushrooms, cleaned, stems removed

1/4 cup vegan parmesan cheese

1/4 cup raw walnuts, crushed

2 cloves garlic, finely minced

1 1/2 Tablespoons olive oil + more for drizzling

Directions

1. Preheat oven to 350 degrees.
2. In a small saucepan, bring vegetable stock to a boil. Add rice. Lower heat, cover and cook until liquid is completely absorbed (about 30-45 minutes). Longer cooking will give softer texture.
3. Meanwhile, toast walnuts in oven for 5 minutes. Set aside.

4. Coat cleaned, de-stemmed mushrooms with olive oil and set aside. Bake the mushrooms on a baking sheet for 10 minutes. Remove from oven.
5. Fluff cooked rice. Add vegan parmesan cheese, toasted walnuts, minced garlic and 1 1/2 Tablespoons olive oil. Stir. Season to taste.
6. Spoon filling into the par-baked mushrooms. Top with additional vegan parmesan cheese and bake again for 15-18 minutes (mushrooms should be tender and the parmesan is golden brown).
7. Serve.

Nutrition Information

Serving size: 1 mushroom
Calories: 66
Total Fat: 4 g
Total Carbohydrate: 8.5 g
Sugars: 0.6 g
Protein: 2.2 g
Sodium: 72 mg

Stuffed Tomatoes

Yield: 2-3 servings

Ingredients

2 medium tomatoes

1/2 small carrot,halved

1/2 celery rib, sliced

1/2 small onion, peeled

2 teaspoons olive oil

1 small garlic clove, peeled

1/4 teaspoon dried oregano

1 tablespoon white wine or vegetable broth

1/3 cup dry bread crumbs

2 tablespoons grated Parmesan cheese

3 to 4 fresh basil leaves, thinly sliced

Directions

1. Prepare tomatoes by slicing off tops. Scoop out the pulp, leaving about 1/2-inch thick shell. Drain shells, cut side down, over paper towels. Set aside pulp and tops.

2. In a food processor, process carrot, celery, onion, garlic and tomato pulp until finely chopped.

3. At this point, preheat oven to 350 degrees and coat a baking dish with cooking spray.

4. Heat the olive oil in a large skillet. Sauté the vegetable mixture over medium heat. Add oregano and cook until tender.

5. Add wine or broth. Keep uncovered while simmering until liquid is reduced by half. Turn off heat and stir in bread crumbs, Parmesan cheese and basil.

6. Spoon filling into tomatoes and replace tops. Bake until heated through (about 15-20 minutes).

Nutrition Information

Serving size: 1
Calories: 182
Total Fat: 7 g
Total Carbohydrate: 23 g
Sugars: 1.8 g
Protein: 6 g
Sodium: 234 mg

Thanksgiving Stuffed Pumpkin

Yield: 4 servings

Ingredients

1 medium pumpkin, about 8 inches in diameter

2 cups cooked wild rice

2 teaspoon olive oil

1 medium onion, minced

3 large cloves garlic, minced

6 mushrooms, chopped

1/2 cup walnut, chopped

1/2 cup dried cranberries

1/4 cup spinach, chopped

1 teaspoon dried oregano

1 teaspoon dried thyme

1 teaspoon ground cumin

Salt& pepper

Directions

1. Preheat oven to 400 degrees.
2. In a skillet, toast walnuts over medium heat for about 2 minutes. Toss continuously. Remove from heat and set aside.
3. Add 1 teaspoon oil to the skillet and sauté onions and garlic until just about to brown. Add mushrooms, cook a minute longer and remove from heat. Allow to cool.
4. Cut off top of pumpkin, cutting along sides and pulling out. Clean out innards and seeds. Brush inside of pumpkin with remaining 1 teaspoon oil. Season generously with salt and pepper.
5. In a large bowl, mix together all ingredients for the filling and transfer to pumpkin cavity. Press down intermittently to pack tightly. Stuff pumpkin until completely filled.
6. Replace pumpkin top. Wrap the whole pumpkin tightly in aluminum foil.
7. Position in the middle of a baking sheet or tray. Bake for 1 hour and a half or until soft. Test by inserting a fork or knife into the side.
8. Take out of oven. Cool for about 5-10 minutes before serving.

Nutrition Information

Serving size: 1
Calories: 234.3
Total Fat: 1.3 g
Total Carbohydrate: 30 g
Sugars: 12 g
Protein: 5.2 g
Sodium: 480 mg

Stuffed Figs with Goat Cheese

Yield: 7-8 medium figs

Ingredients

1 pint fresh figs (7-8 pieces)

1 cup goat cheese

1/2 cup walnuts, toasted and chopped

4 tablespoons honey

2 tablespoons balsamic vinegar

Directions

1. Preheat oven to 350 degrees.
2. Mix together honey and balsamic vinegar until free-flowing.
3. In a bowl, mix together cheese and walnuts.
4. Cut off the fig tops. Make a cross cut into the figs but not all the way through.
5. Fill each fig with about a spoonful of cheese-walnut filling.
6. Drizzle each with honey-vinegar syrup.
7. Place in baking dish and bake just until cheese melts and syrup caramelizes (about 5 minutes).

Nutrition Information

Serving size: 2 figs
Calories: 316
Total Fat: 16.3 g
Total Carbohydrate: 39.8 g
Sugars: 34.1 g
Protein: 8.3 g
Sodium: 109 mg

Stuffed Cabbage

Yield: 6 servings

Ingredients

<u>For sauce</u>

1 medium onion, chopped

1/8 teaspoon baking soda

4 cloves garlic, minced

1 28-ounce can diced fire-roasted tomatoes

116-ounce can diced fire-roasted tomatoes, pureed in blender

1 Tablespoon tomato paste

Salt and pepper

<u>For cabbage filling</u>

1 large cabbage, ragged leaves and core removed

3 cups cooked lentils

1/4 cup raisins

1 cup cooked brown rice

1 medium onion, minced

2 cloves garlic, minced

2 Tablespoons fresh parsley, minced

2 teaspoons lemon juice

1 teaspoon paprika

Salt and pepper

1/4 teaspoon allspice

Directions

For the sauce

1. Using a non-stick pan, cook onions with baking soda over medium heat. When onions have are soft, add garlic and cook 1 minute more. Add remaining sauce ingredients.
2. Reduce heat to very low. Cover and cook for 30 minutes.

For cabbage and filling

1. Preheat oven to 350 degrees and spray a shallow baking dish with non-stick cooking spray.
2. In a pot, boil enough water to cover the cabbage. Immerse the cabbage, core-end

UP, into the boiling water. Cabbage is ready when leaves are soft and begin to separate from the cabbage core.

3. Remove leaves using tongs. Be careful not to tear the leaves. You need 10-12 whole leaves.

4. Drain and rinse the leaves with cold water. Pat dry with paper towels and trim off any thick stem or part of the core at the base of the leaves.

5. Shred the remaining leaves in the pot and add to the sauce. Continue to keep sauce temperature at very low and keep covered.

6. Prepare lentils and remaining ingredients by mixing together in a medium bowl. Season with salt and pepper.

7. Position leaf on table, concave side up. Place 1/3 cup lentil mixture near the stem end. Fold the stem over the filling and then fold the sides toward the middle. Roll up. Place, seam side down, on a shallow baking dish. Repeat with the other leaves.

8. Pour the sauce over the cabbage rolls.

9. Bake for about 50-60 minutes or until sauce is thickened and you see oil rising to the surface of the sauce.

10. Serve drizzled with sauce.

Nutrition Information

Serving size: 2 cabbage rolls
Calories: 356
Total Fat:1.2 g
Total Carbohydrate: 72.3 g
Sugars: 25.4 g
Protein: 18.1 g
Sodium: 1333 mg

DESSERT RECIPES

Truffles

Yield: 24 truffles

Ingredients

1/4 cup coconut milk

2 cups vegan chocolate chips

1/4 cup + 2 Tablespoons coconut oil

1/3 cup cocoa powder, unsweetened

Directions

1. In a double boiler, warm the coconut milk. Stir in the chocolate chips and coconut oil until combined thoroughly.
2. Pour the mixture slowly (to minimize bubbling) into a shallow bowl or container.
3. Refrigerate until chilled through.
4. Use a fruit or melon baller to make small truffles. Coat with cocoa powder.
5. Other possible coatings are dessicated

coconut or crushed nuts.

Nutrition Information

Serving size: 1 truffle
Calories: 103
Total Fat: 6.3 g
Total Carbohydrate: 13.9 g
Sugars: 10.7 g
Protein: 1.6 g
Sodium: 0 mg

Strawberry Ice Cream

Yield: 10 scoops

Ingredients

1 1/2 pounds fresh strawberries, rinsed, hulled and sliced

1/2 cup sugar

2 Tablespoons honey

1 cup plain rice milk

1/2 cup coconut milk

2 teaspoons fresh lemon juice

2 teaspoons kirsch or vodka (optional)

Directions

1. In a bowl, mix the berries, sugar and honey thoroughly. Let stand at room temperature for one hour.
2. Add the rest of the ingredients to the berry mixture and puree using an immersion blender. Puree until smooth. If desired, press through a sieve to remove the seeds.

3. Adjust the taste with lemon juice or liquor, if needed. Liquor helps soften the texture of the ice cream.
4. Chill. For freezing, follow the instructions of your ice cream maker's manufacturer. Note: This is a low-fat ice cream and it may become too firm if frozen for a long time. It's meant to be consumed shortly after churning.

Nutrition Information

Serving size: 1 scoop
Calories: 90
Total Fat: 0.6 g
Total Carbohydrate: 22.2 g
Sugars: 17.2 g
Protein: 0.6 g
Sodium: 14.4 mg:

Vegan Brownies

Yield: 16 pieces

Ingredients

2 cups unbleached all-purpose flour

2 cups white sugar

3/4 cup unsweetened cocoa powder

1 teaspoon baking powder

1 teaspoon salt

1 cup water

1 cup vegetable oil

1 teaspoon vanilla extract

Directions

1. Preheat the oven to 350 degrees.
2. Mix flour, sugar, cocoa powder, baking powder and salt together in a bowl.
3. Pour in water, vegetable oil and vanilla.
4. Mix until well blended and smooth.
5. Spread evenly in a 9x13 inch baking pan.
6. Bake for 25 to 30, or until surface no longer looks shiny.
7. Allow to cool for at least 10 minutes before cutting into squares

Nutrition Information

Serving size: 1
Calories: 280
Total Fat: 14.6 g
Total Carbohydrate: 30.8 g
Sugars: 26 g
Protein: 2.3 g
Sodium: 179 mg

Pumpkin Cheesecake

Yield: 8 slices

Ingredients

<u>For crust</u>

      1 cup dates, pitted (about 20 dates)

      1 1/2 cups walnuts

      Sea salt

<u>For filling</u>

      1 1/2 cups cashews nuts, soaked in very hot water for 1 hour

      1 lemon, juiced

      1/4 cup + 1 Tbsp coconut milk

      3 Tablespoons olive oil

      1/2 cup pure maple syrup

      1/4 cup + 1 Tablespoon pumpkin puree

      Sea salt

      3/4 teaspoon pumpkin pie spice

      1 teaspoon vanilla extract

1/4 teaspoon ground cinnamon

For topping

Coconut whipped cream, optional

Brown sugar pecans, optional

Directions

1. Prepare cashew nuts in advance. Pour boiling hot water to cover the cashews. Leave uncovered and let soak for 1 hour.
2. Chop dates in a blender until fine and sticky. Set aside.
3. Blend walnuts and a pinch of sea salt until meal-like in consistency and only a few large pieces remain. Put the dates back into the blender with the walnuts and blend until it sticks together when squeezed between the thumb and forefinger. A too-crumbly dough needs more dates; while a too-sticky one needs more walnuts. When you've reached the right consistency, set it aside.
4. Line a springform pan with parchment paper, or muffin pans with cupcake liners.
5. Transfer the crust mixture into the pan. Press down with the back of a spoon, pushing some of the mixture

up the sides of the pan. Place in the freezer to set.

6. Drain the cashew nuts and blend. Add the other ingredients for the filling to the blender. Blend until smooth. If the mixture won't smoothen, add small amounts of almond or coconut milk and blend again.

7. Pour the filling into the prepared crust. Tap the pan to release any air bubbles.

8. Cover with plastic wrap and freeze until firm (4-6 hours at least, depending on the size of the pan used).

9. The pie is set if it pops out of the pan easily. If not, return to the freezer.

10. Remove from pan and let thaw for 15 minutes.

11. Serve topped with coconut whipped cream and brown sugar pecans (optional).

.

Nutrition Information

Serving size: 1 serving
Calories: 434
Total Fat: 29.6 g
Total Carbohydrate: 40.1 g
Sugars: 26.7 g
Protein: 9.6 g
Sodium: 72 mg

Apple Crisp

Yield: 10 servings

Ingredients

For filling

8 medium-large apples, peeled, cored, cut into bite-size pieces

1 lemon, juiced

2/3 cup coconut sugar

1 1/2 teaspoons ground cinnamon

3 Tablespoons arrowroot s cornstarch

1/4 cup fresh apple juice

1/2 teaspoon ground ginger

optional: pinch nutmeg

For topping

1 cup rolled oats

1/2 cup almond meal

1/2 cup unbleached all purpose flour

1/2 cup coconut sugar

1/2 cup muscovado sugar

1/2 cup pecans, roughly chopped

1/4 teaspoon sea salt

1 teaspoon ground cinnamon

1/4 cup melted coconut oil

1/4 cup olive oil

Directions

1. Preheat oven to 350 degrees.
2. In a large bowl, combine ingredients for the filling. Mix well. Transfer to a 9-inch by 13-inch baking dish. Spread the filling as evenly as possible.
3. Mix all topping ingredients together in a bowl, breaking any lumps.
4. Pour topping evenly over apple mixture.
5. Bake, uncovered, for about 50 minutes. The apple crisp is done when filling bubbles and topping is deep golden brown.
6. Remove from heat and let cool for 30 minutes before serving.
7. May be served with vegan cream or vegan ice cream.

Nutrition Information

Serving size: 1 serving
Calories: 436
Total Fat: 17.4 g
Total Carbohydrate: 2.1 g
Sugars: 50.8 g
Protein: 4.1 g
Sodium: 49 mg

PB & J Bars

Yield: 9-10 bars

Ingredients

For crust

1 cup gluten-free rolled oats

1 cup raw almonds

1/4 teaspoon sea salt

2 Tablespoon coconut sugar

4 1/2 Tablespoons coconut oil, melted

For filling

3/4 cup vegan strawberry jam

1/2 cup frozen or fresh strawberries, chopped

2 Tablespoon creamy peanut butter, natural salted

Directions

1. Preheat oven to 350 degrees.
2. Line an 8-inchx8-inch baking dish with parchment paper.

3. Combine jam and strawberries in a saucepan. Cook over medium heat until pourable (about 7 minutes). Set aside.
4. Put crust ingredients, EXCEPT coconut oil, into a food processor or blender. Blend into a fine meal, making sure no large pieces remain. Transfer to a mixing bowl.
5. Cut in the melted coconut oil. Mix well until mixture looks like wet sand.
6. Put mixture into baking dish. Spread and press down with the back of a spoon.
7. Bake for 15 minutes. Raise temperature to 375 degrees and cook 5 minutes more. The edges should be turning golden brown. Remove from heat.
8. Reduce oven heat to 350 degrees.
9. While crust is still hot, spread strawberry jam mixture over it. Use a spoon or spatula to spread the jam evenly.
10. Drop teaspoonfuls of peanut butter over the jam layer. Swirl peanut butter and jam together using a spoon.
11. Return to oven and bake for about 10 minutes. Jam should be bubbly.
12. Take out of oven and let cool for 2-3 hours. Remove from pan and cut into bars.

Nutrition Information

Serving size: 1
Calories: 289
Total Fat: 17.1 g
Total Carbohydrate: 31.2 g
Sugars: 18 g
Protein: 5.2 g
Sodium: 59 mg

Vegan Mini Pies

Yield: 24 mini pies

Ingredients

<u>For cakes</u>

1/2 cup unsweetened plain almond milk

3/4 teaspoon apple cider vinegar

1 1/2 teaspoons baking soda

2 flax "eggs" (2 Tablespoons flaxseed meal + 5 Tablespoons water)

1/4 cup grape seed or canola oil

1/3 cup coconut sugar

1/4 cup + 1 Tablespoons pure maple syrup

3/4 cups applesauce, unsweetened

1/2 teaspoon pure vanilla extract

1/4 teaspoon sea salt

1/2 teaspoon baking powder

1/2 cup + 1 Tablespoon cocoa powder, unsweetened

1/2 cup finely ground raw almonds

1/4 cup gluten free oat flour or finely ground raw oats

3/4 cups + 1 Tablespoon gluten-free flour blend

For filling

2 14-ounce cans coconut cream, chilled overnight refrigerator

6 Tablespoons powdered sugar

Directions

1. Whip well-chilled coconut cream with powdered sugar. Transfer to a piping bag and refrigerate to set.
2. Combine almond milk, vinegar and baking soda in a liquid measuring cup. Stir and set aside.
3. Prepare flax "eggs" by combining flaxseed meal and water. Let rest for 5 minutes.
4. Whisk in the oil, coconut sugar, and maple syrup into "eggs." Add applesauce, vanilla and salt. Whisk in almond mixture until thoroughly incorporated.
5. Add baking powder, cocoa powder, almond meal, oat flour, and gluten free flour, and whisk until free from large lumps.
6. Chill batter for 20 minutes to thicken.

7. Meanwhile, preheat oven to 350 degrees. Coat baking sheets with non-stick cooking spray.
8. Scoop batter by the Tablespoonful and drop onto baking sheet, leaving 1-inch space for spreading. Use the spoon to spread dollop into a disc.
9. Bake for 10-15 minutes, or until the edges appear dry. Remove from oven and let rest for 5 minutes.
10. Transfer to cooling racks to cool completely.
11. When you've used up all the batter, you should have about 48 mini cakes.
12. When cakes are completely cooled, pipe a generous amount of coconut whipped cream onto the under-side of 24 cakes. Top with a second mini-cake, like a sandwich.
13. Best served after chilling for 6-8 hours.

Nutrition Information

Serving size: 1
Calories: 170
Total Fat: 11.8 g
Total Carbohydrate: 16.9 g
Sugars: 9.1 g
Protein: 2.4 g
Sodium: 109 mg

Poached Pears

Yield: 4 servings

Ingredients

1 1/2 cups red wine

1 lemon

1 orange, quartered

3/4 cup sugar

1/4 teaspoon vanilla extract

1 cinnamon stick

5 cloves

4 small ripe pears, peeled

Directions

1. Mix the ingredients EXCEPT the pears in a saucepan. Stir.
2. Add the pears and bring to a boil.
3. Reduce heat and simmer, uncovered, for about 25 minutes. Flip the pears occasionally. Pears are done when easily pierced with the tip of a knife.
4. Use a slotted spoon to remove pears from the liquid. Transfer to serving plates.
5. Remove orange quarters and spices from the liquid. Simmer into a syrup (about 15

minutes). The liquid should have been reduced by two-thirds.

6. Serve pears with the syrup.

Nutrition Information

Serving size: 1
Calories: 318
Total Fat: 0
Total Carbohydrate: 66 g
Sugars: 55 g
Protein: 1 g
Sodium: 8 mg

Sweet Rosemary Pears

Yield: 4 servings

Ingredients

3 pears

1/4 cup fresh orange juice

1 Tablespoon chopped fresh rosemary

1/4 cup sugar

Directions

1. Combine the rosemary and sugar.
2. Cut the pears into wedges and arrange on dessert plates.
3. Drizzle with orange juice and sprinkle with sugar-and-rosemary mixture.

Nutrition Information

Serving size: 1
Calories: 177
Total Fat: 0 g
Total Carbohydrate: 46 g
Sugars: 33 g
Protein: 1 g
Sodium: 2 mg

Melon with Sea Salt and Mint

Yield: 8 servings

Ingredients

1 honeydew melon

1/2 cup fresh mint, roughly chopped

1 teaspoon coarse sea salt

Directions

1. Scoop the fruit using a fruit baller, or cut into bite-size cubes.
2. Distribute into serving bowls or cups.
3. Sprinkle mint and salt over the melon just before serving.

Nutrition Information

Serving size: 1 serving
Calories: 46
Total Fat: 0 g
Total Carbohydrate: 12 g
Sugars: 10.7 g
Protein: 1 g
Sodium: 215 mg

Other books from IronRingPublishing.com

Visit <u>IronRingPublishing.com</u> to sign up for notifications of new releases, free books, and other special giveaways!

Princess Wiggly – Exercise and Healthy Eating For Kids

This entertaining story tells how **Princess Wiggly** frees children from the unhealthy influences of the lazy-loving **Couch Potato** and his trouble-making sidekick, the **Slug Monster.**

Pick up a paperback copy from
IronRingPublishing.com for a gift to some
Munchkins you love!

ABOUT THE AUTHOR

Dan DeFigio is the bestselling author of **Beating Sugar Addiction For Dummies**, **Princess Wiggly**, **Beach Games For Kids!**, and other books. Dan has been one of the most respected experts in the fitness and nutrition fields since 1993. He has been featured on CNN's Fit Nation, The Dr. Phil Show, SELF Magazine, along with an array of other TV, radio, and print outlets.

Low Sugar Snacks

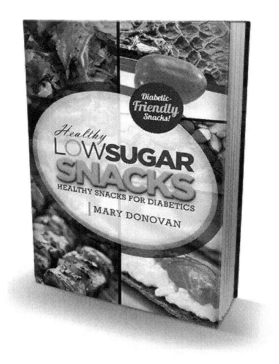

Do you have trouble keeping your sugar under control?

Are you struggling to lose weight?

LOW SUGAR SNACKS to the rescue!

Healthy, low-glycemic snacks are a vital part of keeping your blood sugar stable.

Recipe specialist Mary Donovan has prepared a collection of delicious, low-sugar snacks especially for diabetics.

Included are both cooking and no-cook recipes for you to stay stocked with healthy, low sugar foods to eat whenever you need a boost.

Get your copy from IronRingPublishing.com!

Disclaimer and Terms of Use

The author and the publisher do not hold any responsibility for errors, omissions, or interpretation of the subject matter herein, and specifically disclaim any responsibility for the safety or appropriateness of any dietary advice or recipe preparation presented in this book. This book is presented for informational purposes only. Always consult a qualified health care practitioner before beginning any dietary regimen or before using any nutrition supplements.